This Is Who We Are

Tales of the McCamus Family
Beverly McCamus Toppin

The best to you!
Bev Toppin

THE LEARNING CENTER
1ST CONGREGATIONAL CHURCH
UCC ANOKA

Copyright 2017 by Beverly McCamus Toppin

All rights reserved.

ISBN: 1545122628

The tales are as I remember them and are an expression of the character of the family. Errors are not intentional.

To my daughters and my grandchildren who descend from the McCamus Family

With gratitude to all who helped me tell the stories of those who came before.

Thanks to Nicole Varichak, June Anderson, Todd Anderson, and all the relatives who went before me.

FORWARD

The McCamus Family came from Ulster, Ireland to Ontario, Canada. It is in many ways a common story. The individuals in the tales are, however, are unique personalities who made their own paths. Some stayed in Canada and some moved to the United States. The stories are interwoven with the history of the countries in which they lived. They were shaped by the events that occurred and they made their lives as they confronted the challenges that came before them. They were very human and lived very human lives and passed on their characters to their progeny.

TABLE OF CONTENTS

1	BELONGING
2	EIRE
6	COUNTY CAVAN, ULSTER, IRELAND
9	CAVAN COUNTY, ONTARIO, CANADA
18	GREAT-GRANDMOTHER ELIZABETH
25	SAMUEL MCCAMUS
27	GREAT IN EVERY WAY
30	ROWE MCCAMUS
37	ELIZA BRANT MCCAMUS
41	CONFLAGRATION
50	THE YEAR WAS 1933
57	TINY
63	MY AUNT MARGE
71	MY AUNT VERONA
74	DADDY
85	MOTHER
93	MY LITTLE SISTER BARB
103	TREPIDATION
110	ME
135	DON
146	KAKA
150	MY DAUGHTER EILENE
155	NANCY
162	GRATITUDE

Our family at the farm in Winnebago.

BELONGING

I am so peculiar to myself. That is why I write these stories of our family and where we came from and how we lived. I hope to somehow find out why I am as I am. It is a great mystery never to be solved, of course, but what shall I do with my odd person? It is a very self-centered search. I have never figured out how to go beyond myself and my own perceptions, my own feelings, my own being. As they say, "Everywhere I go, there I am."

In Romans in the Bible, Paul states, "I do not understand my own actions. For I do not what I want, but I do the very thing I hate."

I want to belong, to fit in, or do I? Sometimes I almost manage to fit in, but my thoughts go elsewhere. I do not like the book that everyone else likes. I have wide and eclectic tastes in food, in style, and in people. I am easily bored and I am drawn to the exotic and different as long as it is not dangerous or unwholesome. I like variety and expanse and inclusion. I think these thoughts are not unusual. They are human thoughts. Maybe I am not as odd as I think am. Here is the part of the McCamus family story, that family from which I descend.

EIRE

I want to go back to the beginning. As I see it far too briefly, here is how it all began. "Sin sceal Ella." (Shin skale ella.) That's another story." Seemingly there are a million stories.

Twelve thousand years of Irish history. I don't even know how to begin. The early settlers came in the middle stone age. There is the bog man who lived somewhere between 362B.E. and 175 B.E. His body was found somewhat intact preserved by the peat land in the bogs of Ireland. There were the Picts. There were the Gaels. There were the Celts. There were the Vikings. There were the Normans. There were the Huguenots. There were the Quakers. There were, of course, the Scots, and Brits. There are all those heroes and all those battles to try to free Ireland.

Four point two million people live in Ireland today. The land in area is less than the state of Minnesota. There are approximately forty million people of Irish descent in the United States. The Irish names abound; O'Neil, Flaherty, O'Connell, Donohue, and Farrell. There is a back and forth and toing and froing between Ireland and the U.S. and back. The Irish come and bring their culture, which is modified and returned, as for instance the dancing. The Irish brought the jig and their own folk dancing to America. It was changed and we created square dancing and line dancing. And the Irish took it back and changed it once again and it became River Dance.

This Is Who We Are

There is an American Festival in Ireland and Irish Festivals in many places in America. We celebrate St. Patrick's Day. We sing Irish music and American music about Ireland. We tear up when "Danny Boy" is played and sung, at least some of us do. The Irish adulate American politicians who have Irish heritage as the Kennedys, the Clintons have, and they adore George Mitchell who worked out the peace agreement in Northern Ireland.

First of all, Ireland is a country of indescribable beauty. It is an island and surrounded by the sea. The craggy coast and the wild waves and tides and time beat and wash up and flow and shape the land. There are cliffs like the Cliffs of Moher from which the Aran Islands can be seen. Just a bit of a leap is the Cliff of the Foals. As the story goes from this cliff a group of young fairy horses leaped and remained to run the rocks.

There are the mountains, not high, high mountains, but rocky peaks that sometimes are revealed through the clouds. They have colorful, poetic names. The Sleive Mish, are the Mountains of Mystery. The Macgillicuddy Reeks are the Black Mountains.

Then there is the green. "Forty Shades of Green" is the song written, surprisingly, by Johnny Cash. Eighty per cent of the Irish people are still farmers. The fields are small and lush and the pastures are filled with cattle and sheep. The trees were cut long ago, but the Irish government has a launched a program to reforest the land especially on the hillsides and the land that isn't easily farmed. There seem to be at least forty shades of green.

The Irish weather produces rain and clouds and fog and mist. "A misty, moisty morning," said a traveler. In this gossamer, gauzy world it is easy to see ghosts and spirits and unnatural creatures of the imagination. There is the Pooka, who has many shapes. Sometimes he is a horse, then an ass, then a bull, then a goat and now an eagle. He is the basis, it is thought, for Puck, the character in Shakespeare's *Midsummer Night's Dream*. There are the banshees who are women and fairies that follow old families and wail before a death. They wail and sing in chorus in an unearthly screech that could only portend despair and death. And, of course, there are the leprechauns, the fairy shoemakers.

The signs in Ireland are in two languages, English and Gaelic. The Irish have saved their culture by saving their language. Gaelic is taught in the schools. In some parts of Ireland, particularly in the Southwest it is the prevailing language. There is a Gaelic TV station. Songs are sung in Gaelic and many Gaelic phrases are used even in the English speaking parts of Ireland. There is the "cead mile failte" (kaid meela foil'tche), which means "a hundred thousand welcomes". Hello is "Dia guit" (Deea gwith), which literally means "God be with you". A toast is "slante" (slawn'tche) meaning "your health".

The culture of Ireland has been radiated throughout the world. Some of the very best writers in the world come from Ireland. Consider James Joyce, George Bernard Shaw, Oscar Wilde, and the poets, William Butler Yeats and Seamus Heaney.

Irish education and culture are not surpassed. The schools are actually run by the Catholic Church. Since the country is 95% Catholic this does not cause a problem. There are private schools as well, but they are not free as the Catholic public system is.

The best thing about Ireland is her people. They are honest in spite of all that blarney. They are generous. They are hospitable. They are kind, mostly. Exclude the Troubles, the conflict in Northern Ireland. They are industrious. They are tenacious. Of course, this also means stubborn. They are loyal. They are amorous. They are charitable. They are imaginative. They are spiritual. One could do much worse that celebrate one's Irish heritage.

There is no Better poet, especially if one is old, to follow than Yeats, crazy Yeats, when he writes in "Sailing to Byzantium":

> "An aged man is but a paltry thing ,
> A tattered coat upon a stick,
> Unless soul clap its hands and sing, and louder sing."

COUNTY CAVAN, ULSTER, IRELAND

Great great grandmother, Jane was a McIndoo who came from Cavan County, Ulster, Ireland in the early 1800's. She met and married Robert McCamus who came from the same place.

It is amusing to me that name of the town from which they migrated was called Shercock. It came from the Gaelic Irish name Searcog. The families were Scots-Irish, these ancestors of mine. They were Protestant and probably Presbyterian with a strong straight laced Calvinistic bent. Thus I laughed when I discovered the very risqué meaning of the old Irish name. It means "young love," Shercock after all.

There is much to be learned about the area from which they came. They immigrated to Canada, to Cavan County, Ontario, where there were already McCamuses in the early 1800's before the War of 1812. Why did they leave and settle in such a wild and uninhabited place? I will never know exactly, of course, but I have some guesses.

My father always called our heritage Scots-Irish. He made a joke of this, by saying he did not know if he was of Scot or Irish descent. He did suspect, however, that he must be Irish, since he had never been able to hang on to a dime and the Scots were the thrifty ones.

I did not realize that there is a category of nationalities that is actually called Scots-Irish. This is what we must be, I think. It goes back in history to the old conflicts of both

Scotland and Ireland with English rule. It reaches backward to the time of James I and Henry VIII. The Irish were always a challenge to the British monarchy. A plan was devised and passed on that emigrants from England and Scotland be placed in Northern Ireland to dilute and tame the wild Irish who lived there. This was called the plantation and included counties in Northern Ireland. Among the counties was Cavan. By 1640 one hundred thousand Scots had settled in Ireland. This was far more than the 40,000 English who arrived there. The geography of Northern Ireland favored the Scots and the Scottish temperament was more suitable to the rigors of living in Ulster. The Scots brought with them new modes of farming. The Irish had mostly raised livestock and moved from place to place to graze them. The Scots cleared and tilled the land. They also followed strictly the Calvinistic doctrines they carried with them.

The English did not end their animosity toward either the Scots or the Irish with the Plantation System . The English Anglicans discriminated not only against the Irish Catholics, but also against the Scot Presbyterians. In the many conflicts that arose the Scottish population was decimated. They were either killed or decided to escape by emigrating to the United States . There were few Scots left in Northern Ireland by the late 1600's.

Then in 1700 a new wave of plantation residents were sent to Northern Ireland. These came to be known as the Scots-Irish. They rented and farmed the land. In Cavan County, this land was known as "drumlin country," because the landscape contained small hills and lakes which were formed in the last Ice Age. The main crop was flax which was used in linen making.

Most of the land at this time was owned by absentee landlords. In their greedy desire for more money, they decided to raise the rents. The farmers could no longer eke out a subsistence living and so by 1771, they began leaving for the New World to make a living. The conditions continued well into the beginning of the nineteenth century when the McCamuses left for Canada. They suffered religious discrimination as well as economic deprivation.

This anonymous statement descries the Scots-Irish of the time.

"Though loyal to the crown, they were a people who, through decades of adversity, had become self-reliant, and never quite lost the feeling they were surrounded by a hostile world."

These were my ancestors who ended up in Cavan County, Ontario, Canada in the early 1800's.

CAVAN COUNTY, ONTARIO, CANADA

I don't know my great great great grandfather's name. He was the youngest of several brothers. The others are named in the family tree, but my ancestor's name was lost.

Some of the McCamus family who lived in County Cavan, Ulster, had already immigrated to Cavan County, Ontario, at the early part of the nineteenth century. Robert McCamus, my great great grandfather came over on the boat with Jane McIndoo who was my great great grandmother. They were young then and they married after they arrived in Ontario. Already in Ontario was Robert's cousin who was also named Robert. He and his family had settled around Peterborough and this was where they made their home. It must have been wooded at that time, but when the trees were cleared it was fertile farm land.

What was and is our connection to the forest? It was to the Canadian forest that the people came. It is as if some long buried Druid green umbilical cord tethered us to the pines as mother and as home. The draw is still the wooded places.

And there were the water, the lakes, and the rivers. Water always has meaning.

I have written a totally imaginary interview with Jane McIndoo. She has been lost more or less in the archives. There were a lot of McIndoos back in Ireland and some of them immigrated to Canada. I have great admiration for Jane McIndoo. She and Robert McCamus are my lineage. I think she must have been a woman of magnificent strength, physically, mentally, emotionally and spiritually. I am very proud to have her as an ancestor.

This is my pretend conversation with her.

"I did not have time to be lonely. Robert and I had to carve a farm and home in that new world wilderness. Canada was not a country at the time. It was a colony of Great Britain. We had assistance, of course, from the other McCamuses and from our neighbors, but there seemed endless labor.

We had come with our parents from Ireland. It was a new start in a magnificent open country filled with forests and water and land and all kinds of adventure. The majestic white pines and the red maples and the birch and aspen were our guardians and our protectors stretching above us like a roof. I think of the old battle of the trees of long ago. That is really a Welsh poem, but it fits. Such strength and power did they wield and they held a spiritual connection with all of creation. They embodied life and seemed to touch heaven.

We came from County Cavan, Ulster, Ireland to Cavan County, Ontario, Canada. In some ways they were the same. They both had forests and rivers. Both challenged us to live in circumstances difficult and toilsome. They both were lusciously green, verdant, and wild.

Trees and water were our hope and our faith and our religion from long ago. There were the rivers and the lakes all connecting and providing us with easy ways of getting around. Ontario means 'beautiful water' and there are the thousands of bodies of water from the streams and brooks and ponds to the Great Lakes to prove that it is truly a descriptive name.

'Why did we leave Ireland?' you ask. We left before the potato famine and the surge of immigration to the United States and Canada merely to survive. Why did we leave? Was it for adventure? Was it for new opportunity? Was it because we were Protestant in a largely Catholic country? Was it an economic decision? Did Ireland not have land for everyone? Was it because our cousins had already settled in Cavan County, Ontario? Why did we come? Was it ambition? Or was it escape from intolerance?

We came for perhaps all of those reasons and also the fighting. Never forget the fighting. There was always the underlying tension, the discord, the eruption of violence. There was always the threat of famine. Even before the great potato famines and the emigration in the middle of the nineteenth century, there was hunger and dependence on the crops and lack of land. There was plenty of land and opportunity in Canada.

I, of course, was a child. I did not make the decision to leave Ireland. I came along for the ride. I give you answers of my father and mother. I was happy we had come. I had no desire to return to Ireland. That I leave to my progeny who seem to find the land and people there so romantic and exciting. It was beautiful and it had its charms, but life is hard wherever and whenever you live it.

Of course, nothing is ever really pure and feelings are ambivalent. We also had to cut those beautiful trees to clear the land and remove stumps and pick up the huge boulders that prevented us from farming. We had to farm. We had to produce our own food. We had to produce almost everything ourselves.

Wheat was the crop of choice in southern Ontario. The land was productive and raised prolific crops. The wheat was taken into town and ground into flour to provide food and substance for our thirteen children. However, other occupations had to undertaken. Lumbering was an obvious choice. Felling trees and sawing them for the builders who were coming to settle the areas was the occupation in the winter. There was construction as well, construction of a dam, construction of roads the building of houses. We cut the trees. Robert built the house and the sheds himself. He had to be a carpenter and the buildings stood long after he died so suddenly.

You ask if I became just too weary and too tired to go on. I didn't lie awake on my pillow and toss and turn for wanting the gods of sleep to come. When I was young and there was one child and then another, another, and another, I was full of life and hope and I seemed to have unending strength and vigor. God did not give me thirteen children for no reason.

Then there was the day that Robert had his fatal heart attack. He had gone out to the barn to take care of the cattle. James found him. He was lucky in that he went quickly. It was not lucky for the rest of us, of course. It was fortunate that William had completed his medical training and he could take me and the youngest children into his household. Oh, for some loneliness.

It was as God planned it, I guess. When Robert and I were first married, we did not think we would have thirteen children. We had no idea of what was to come. No one ever does. Life surprises everyone. We went to church every Sunday. We began when we first came here to Cavan County, Ontario, to have prayer meetings in our homes. We needed God. Sunday was a day of rest.

Religion was always important to us. We were Irish Protestants and firmly held our beliefs to counter the strength of the Catholics who really outnumbered us. Our religion was a strict religion. There was duty, a lot of work, and there were a lot of unwritten rules to follow. I did this more because my circumstances forced me to follow the rules than that I found them helpful. I had thirteen children to raise. This did not allow anything but following the rules. We attended the Methodist Church faithfully and followed its strictures with care.

And we could talk. Robert and I talked all the time. A lot of it was about the work or about the children or about the church or about the neighbors. We didn't talk about philosophy or theology or religion very much. We took things as thy came. We didn't delve deeply into places where we really had no knowledge.

I was just tired at the end. There were so many children. There was so much work. There was so little time. Finally all my emotion left me in a sort of weary acceptance and unwillingness to fight alone. When Robert died I died too. I did not actually die, of course. I lived on with our son William in Bobcaygeon. It was a comfortable enough life. He was a doctor and a pharmacist who sold patent medicines.

William was born in 1840. He went to college and then to medical school. He graduated from Victoria University in 1869 and he interned at Long Island College Hospital and Bellevue Hospital in New York. He advertised as a physician a surgeon and an accoucheur which is an obstetrician. He came to Peterborough and then went to Bobcaygeon, where he did all kinds of things. He opened a pharmacy and advertised himself as a 'Dealer in Drugs'. He also taught at a local school until they could find a qualified teacher. He made money and helped people, too.

Bobcaygeon is a watery place. It is located on a series of Finger Lakes, which are connected by canals. The water was an early means of transportation, in fact almost the sole transportation at first. Later the lakes provided recreation and vacation travel for the residents of this part of Canada. A system of locks and dams was built there. It is in the area that is called the Kawartha Lakes Region. The First Nation Mississauga named it Kawartha, which means 'bright waters and happy lands'. The system of lakes and rivers goes from Peterborough south and north. It takes in a dozen lakes and the Otonabee, Scugog, Squaw, Mississagua, and Burnt Rivers. Boats traveled between the communities of Bobcaygeon, Fenelon Falls, and Lindsay, Port Perry, and Bridgenorth.

Champlain visited the site of Bobcaygeon in about 1613. He described it in his journal and called it Beaubocage. He found the forests the finest he had seen. He was looking for a post for trading furs and thought this would be an excellent choice. The Mississaugo Indians called it the name which Champlain called it, but the strange name was interpreted by the white English settlers as Bob-cajeon-unk, Bob Cajione. This was their version of the shallow waters name that the natives had bestowed upon it.

It was in Bobcaygeon William met and married Catherine. Her father had arrived from Ireland as we had. They had two sons. Walter died in infancy and is buried in the Bobcaygeon cemetery. He was not two months old. It was a common story losing children. I was fortunate. I was strong and healthy and so were my children.

William and Catherine were good Methodists. William was on the church board. His son William Edward was even more taken with religion. He went to the Philippines as a missionary and never returned to Canada. My daughter, Mary, his aunt, accompanied him and remained there as well. She never married, but devoted her life to the church.

William loved the rivers and so he purchased the boat. Since he was very enterprising he sold fares and used it as a money making venture. His first boat was the Bella Fair. Then he bought a larger vessel to compete on the waters of the region. This boat was called the Columbia. Sometimes he captained it himself. It ran twice a week between Chemong Station and Lakefield. The Colombia was a steamer, which cost $13,000 when it was first built. That was a lot of money in those times. It was a competitor to the ship that was called the Crandella. It was a losing proposition as a business venture. The two ships vied with one another cutting their fares so that neither of them was making any money. The fare from Sturgeon Bay to Lindsay was cut from forty cents to thirty cents to twenty cents and neither ship was making money. Eventually the Columbia had a fire and burned as was the fate of many of the boats on the lakes at the time.

Our daughter Ann Jane was born 1843. As the oldest daughter she was my helper. She cared for the younger children as they were born. She married Henry Scott and moved to Wisconsin. They had six children, Holton Henry, Ernest A, Matilda May, Margaret, Henry A.G.S. and Charlotte. Ann Jane is buried in Mt. Hope Cemetery in Ashland, Wisconsin.

James lived and farmed in Stephenson Township in the Peterborough area his whole life. He was married to Alice Rummerfield and they had four children who all died in childhood. Both James and Alice lived into advanced age. He was 87 when he died and she almost reached 100.

Robert was the next son. He married and lived in Monahan County. Then followed the birth of Margaret. She married Sherman Wesley Minthorne. The Minthornes lived in St. Catherine's Ontario. Rowe McCamus visited them with his Uncle Tom after Eliza died. Marjorie Minthorne wrote letters to Isobel Filmore, who had done the genealogy of the the McCamus family.

Samuel was next in the family number six. He was my great grandfather. He married Elizabeth Rowe who was of English descent. Rowe and May were their children.

Following Samuel was Moses who moved west to Saskatchewan. He sold land at Indianhead, Saskatchewan and gave the money to Samuel.

Elizabeth also lived in Saskatchewan. She was married to a man named Dixon.

John lived in Hurley, Wisconsin. Anna Jane Davis was his wife. They had no children.

Mary went with her younger brother Edward to the Philippines where they were missionaries.

In between Mary and Edward were Thomas and Sarah. Thomas worked as a pharmacist for a while with William in Bobcaygeon. He then went to northern Ontario where he discovered and owned cobalt and copper mines. He was married twice and both his wives died. He had no children. Many years later when Tom was in his ninties Rowe visited him in New Liskerd, Ontario. Tom had also started a telephone company in the area and owned it after he sold the mines.

Samuel Rowe's father who was Ronald's grandfather married Elizabeth Rowe. There is a picture of her taken in Guelph,

Ontario. She was of English extraction and possessed an irascible temper. Rowe's volatile temper was claimed by his daughters to have been inherited from her. Rowe's sister May apparently was the unfortunate victim of their strict unbending rigid ideas about women and what they should allowed to do.

GREAT-GRANDMOTHER ELIZABETH

I didn't want to go. It wasn't that I wasn't curious. I was. It's just that I knew almost nothing about her. She came from England. My Aunt Tiny who was named after her, Elizabeth, but always was called by her nickname Tiny, talked about her quite derisively. Tiny always said she had an impossible temperament and no one much liked her. Everyone blamed my grandfather Rowe's temperament on her. He was equally miserable and disliked. My mother often said I was just like Rowe. This was no compliment and I hated it. I wasn't even sure what her first name was. I did know that my grandfather had been given her last name. That was why he was Rowe McCamus. The name Rowe was my father's middle name, Ronald Rowe McCamus.

It was my daughter, Eilene, who found her. Eilene is very interested in genealogy. She even located a distant relative who was related on Elizabeth's mother's side. Elizabeth's mother was Alice Grose. The family came from Cornwall down on the southwest corner of England on the Celtic Sea not far from Wales. This explains why I have my wild imagination. If my relatives are Irish and Cornish on the McCamus side of the family and my grandmother on my mother's side was named Anna Grimm and my grandfather was of Native American descent there is just no hope that I would not turn out to be strange.

Now when you envision my daughter do not think about me. It is true we look somewhat alike. She has gray hair at 53, too. She is, however, by whatever quirk of DNA a chemical engineer with great confidence and great practical abilities. Children do have two parents. Did I mention she also has limitless energy? Her plans for the trip were expansive and detailed, researched and printed out, step by step. She seemed not to recognize my reluctance and she completely ignored my apprehension about the strenuousness of the journey. There was no way out of the adventure. I had to go whether I wanted to or not.

This was fortunate as it turned out. I was fearful of a crowded and frenzied London. Suffering from jetlag and entering the intimidating Heathrow Airport we made our way on the Heathrow Express and took a bus to Central London where Eilene had found a hotel that was almost affordable. We had arrived in the morning about 10 a.m. and so our room was not ready. The hotel manager put us on the third floor in a room so tiny that there was not room enough to open our luggage. Did I mention I had violated my own rule and took my large suitcase and packed everything I owned. I must have been trying to sabotage myself.

Since we both believe in proceeding as quickly as possible into the local time, we immediately started to follow Eilene's elaborate plans. It was rainy and windy and cold as I was promised it would be. Nevertheless we headed for the Tower of London. We caught on with a Beef Eaters Outdoor Tour and viewed the grassy knoll where Queen Anne Boleyn was beheaded. One of the other tour members, who were few in number, asked if there wasn't sleet in that rain. The Beef

Eater agreeably commented that yes, it could be. It was cold enough. We proceeded to the White Tower. It contained the eleventh century Chapel of St. John the Evangelist and the armor of three hundred years of British kings. This was what Eilene really wanted to see. Henry the Eighth was a large man for the times. He was over six feet tall and his armor was impressive. Some of this was of interest to me as I had just completed reading the second volume of Hilary Mantel's trilogy of novels, *BringUp the Bodies*. It was about Thomas Cromwell who served as minister to Henry VIII.

We did see the crown jewels because, luckily, the weather was so bad there was no queue. We walked right in. The gold and the jewels of royalty are awing, but I have never been much interested in diamonds, rubies, emeralds, and pearls. I have been just too poor, I guess.

The next day was better. We had slept and the rain had momentarily disappeared. Westminster Cathedral was our first joy of the day. An English Gothic Cathedral of great beauty, it is also the burial site of many of the kings of England and a great tour of English history. Henry III built the Cathedral in honor of his hero Edward the Confessor who was canonized as a saint.

It was Oliver Cromwell who began the burial of famous and creative English commoners. Charles Darwin is buried there and many of my favorite poets, John Keats, W.H. Auden, T.S. Eliot among them. Charles Dickens is buried there. The Unknown Warrior from World War I is also commemorated there.

It was the site of royal weddings. The present Queen Elizabeth and Prince Phillip were married there as were Prince William and Catherine Middleton. Queen Elizabeth's coronation was also there.

On we went on foot to the Tate Museum of Art. We viewed many royal portraits, but most impressive was our viewing of William Blake's original illustrations. The room in which they were displayed was dimly lit and there was the story of Job as Blake portrayed it.

"They're changing the guard at Buckingham Palace

And Christopher Robin went down with Alice."

The lines of A.A. Milne we quoted as we walked to the Palace. We watched the ancient pageantry along with the teeming crowds even though it was a cool and cloudy February day. But most interesting was our conversation with an Italian couple nearby. We insisted their nine-year-old daughter have our prime spot near the spiked fence. The children must see the ceremony. Her father worked for an international company and travelled often the U.S. and spoke perfect English. His wife struggled a bit but entered the conversation as well. London is the cosmopolitan city of the world as all cities are now becoming.

We wanted to see a theatre production while in London. We chose *Wicked*, mostly because it was a favorite of my oldest granddaughter. She belongs to my oldest daughter, Kathy. So we took the amazing tube to the Apollo Victory Theatre. A lightweight musical spin off of *The* Wizard of Oz, it was delightful and I did not fall asleep as I feared I might.

Eilene loves to shop. We had to go to Harrods. I felt very midwestern dowdy as we walked through the locked glass cases of jewelry and designer dresses displayed throughout the store. It was Sunday and we reached the bookstore. I purchased a newspaper, the *London Times*, which was placed in a Harrod's bag. Then we headed for our hotel to meet our English relative, David Wharton. He was slight man in his sixties. He had brought his lap top computer with him. We walked to a nearby cafe and ordered an English Tea with scones and clotted cream. We figured out that we were fourth cousins, sharing a connection with Alice Grose, our great great grandmother. When you have so few relatives as I have, it is a great thrill to find a distant cousin. I do have my daughters and grandchildren, of course, but there are almost no relatives of my vintage left. I do believe that I am the most fortunate member of my extended family. David had lost his job during the recession. On top of that his wife had early onset Alzheimers and he had cared for her until she died at age 54. David gave us Cornwall leads to our great-great-grandmother's home there. This had been an important reason for us to travel to England.

Our trip to Cornwall was also one of my great trepidations. The reason is that Eilene insisted on renting a car at Heathrow and driving out of London. We were provided a small Hyundai with automatic shift and a GPS. Now Eilene is very capable, but this driving on the wrong side of the road out of London seemed like a stretch for anyone's abilities. I closed my eyes and tried not to gasp at any close calls. We made it to Salisbury and the bed and breakfast where we stayed. It was then on to Newquay, which is pronounced by the locals as Newkey.

To our surprise the sun was shining and it was 50 degrees above zero Fahrenheit. The Legacy Hotel Victoria was on the water and we could go out on an ancient large balcony and view the cliffs and the ocean. It was tourister's dream. Newquay is a popular resort and a vacation destination for many citizens of the British Isles. It was full of tourists even in February as it was half holiday for the school children and they had the week off from school. We walked through the town and stopped in at St. Michael's Anglican Church. It is an imposing building in Cornish style. We walked in the park bordering the ocean and watched two or three surfers riding the waves even in the temperatures in the 40's Fahrenheit. We also shopped a bit. We needed new umbrellas. Eilene's had almost been blown inside out in London and mine had holes in it.

Our destination for the day, however was Camelford. It was in this area that my great grandmother Elizabeth lived with her parents Francis Barton Rowe and Alice Grose. Alice's father, Captain John Grose, was a miner. Early on, Cornwall prospered because of its tin, copper, and lead mines. The title, Captain, was not a military title, but the title for the mine supervisor. Captain Grose was an official in a lead mine. Tragically, he was killed when he fell down a mine shaft.

Francis Barton Rowe and Alice and some of their children later emigrated to Ontario, Canada. This was where Elizabeth met and married my great-grandfather, Samuel McCamus. Interestingly Francis and Alice returned to Cornwall and were buried there. I don't believe Elizabeth saw them after they returned to Great Britain. Near Camelford are the ruins of a castle purported to be the home of King Arthur, but this is myth.

My cousin, David Wharton, also told us about Bogee Farm. Alice Rowe's mother remarried after Captain John's fatal accident. She married a farmer and Alice and Elizabeth visited the farm often. It is still a working enterprise although it was long ago sold and no family members are a part of the operation. It was interesting to Eilene and to me because we lived on a farm in Minnesota for so many years.

Cornwall is very boggy and Bodwin Moor is close. It has rolling grassy hills, however, and is good pasture land for dairy cows and sheep. Cornwall is known for its clotted cream.

The GPS, somewhere along the way, took us on a one lane road. The hedgerows almost touched the car. We thought it would be a short distance, but it turned out to be longer and more exciting than we had thought. We met a small car. We backed up to a small indentation in the hedgerow and the car crept past us. That was not to be the end of this escapade. We then met a small utility vehicle and stopped, knowing not what to do. It was a government vehicle and fortunately the driver did know the procedure. He backed up some distance to a somewhat wider indentation in the hedgerow and we sneaked by with perhaps a piece of paper between the vehicles.

One of our destinations was St. Ervans. The church we wished to see there was the church where my greats, Francis Barton Rowe and Alice Grose were married. It is an old stone Methodist church and still holds services. The English poet, John Bejetman had bicycled there and written a poem in its honor. Snow drops were immerging in the church garden and a few brave daffodils raised their heads.

There is much more to the trip, but at this point I only wish to say that I am so grateful that I had seen Cornwall where my great-grandmother Elizabeth had lived. I feel differently toward her now. I would have loved to meet her and talk with her. She must have been a very strong, independent, and opinionated woman. She also had a terrible temper which I also share. In learning about her I have learned much about myself. We are strange birds but we had some characteristics that were valuable despite this.

SAMUEL MCCAMUS

I don't know very much about this great-grandfather of mine. I know more about the McCamus family than I know of him. He was number six of the thirteen children, of course. Sometimes with so many, the middle gets lost. I do have a picture of him. My shirttail relative, Isobel Filmore, commented when I showed her the photograph that he looked much like a McCamus. I don't think he was very tall. He looks a bit stern.

What do I know about him? I think perhaps he was a carpenter. I don't know how he and Elizabeth Rowe met. It was probably in Ontario since they both lived there. They went to Michigan for a time because my grandfather Rowe was born there, at least I think so. They also lived for a time in Toronto back in Canada, because that is where Rowe went to school through the fifth grade. She must have died shortly after that as Rowe was only twelve at the time.

Samuel must have been good with money, because that seems to be a McCamus characteristic. Not that any of the McCamus family was rich, except maybe William or Thomas, but the members of the family seemed to be intelligent and handled their financial affairs easily. Samuel had bought some land in St. Louis County and this is where Rowe and Eliza retreated at one time after the Cloquet Fire of 1918. He also perhaps helped Rowe start the newspaper in Brookston and perhaps it was also Samuel's money in the bank there. Most of this is guess-work as neither my father nor my aunts spoke much about him.

Samuel remarried after Elizabeth died. I don't know the name of the woman he married, but they lived in Spokane, Washington. The family visited there on a motor trip in the twenties probably. There is a picture of a woman identified as Grandma McCamus. She is posed with two other women.

I think Samuel and Elizabeth were very strict with their children and it must have been particularly Samuel as Elizabeth died so young. My father Ronald mentions in a letter about his Aunt May after her sad ending that she was never able to do anything she wanted to do.

GREAT IN EVERY WAY

Great-Grandmother Jennie Boyles Brant Gable

She was born Jennie Jessie Boyles. The Boyles family came from Ireland to the United States way back in the 1800's. Some of the Boyles were prominent around Cork in Ireland. Her family was probably not one of them. Jennie's great-grandfather, John Boyles, was born in Ireland in 1771. He moved to the United States to the State of Pennsylvania.

Jennie's father, Samuel Boyles, was a minister. He was a Protestant and probably so was the rest of the family. Ireland is and was very Catholic so this may have been another reason for the move to the United States. The trajectory of the Boyles family was from Pennsylvania to Michigan and from Michigan to Wisconsin.

The trajectory of the Brant family into which Jennie was to marry was from Pennsylvania to Indiana to Wisconsin.

It is a coincidence, or perhaps even more, that both the Witmers, who were Don Toppin's great-grandparents, and the Boyles and the Brants all found themselves in Green County, Wisconsin. However, they were in different areas and their lives took different directions. Both sides of the family did have unhappy situations which constructed their lives. The Witmers, or Witwers as was their real Swiss name, ended up in one of the all too common poor houses of the time in the northern part of the county. That was when their children changed their name to Witmer.

Jennie Boyles Brant lived on the State Line Road in the southern portion of the county dividing Wisconsin and Illinois after she and Franklin Brant were married. It was here that her three daughters were born and the last was Eliza, Ronald McCamus's mother. Frank Brant struggled to make a living for his family. It is thought that he might have been a house painter since he died of lead poisoning. It may be that, instead, he was a farmer who also worked in the county adjoining Monroe in the lead mines near New Diggings, Lafayette County, Wisconsin. Many farmers often supplemented their incomes by working in the declining lead mines.

A lead poisoning death is excruciatingly painful. Jennie must have been his caretaker in this terrible time of trial. She was left a widow with three young daughters when Franklin died. I would very much have liked to talk to her. My grandmother, Eliza, was very intelligent and very capable. She must have learned much from her mother, Jennie.

Jennie was very self-sufficient. Somehow, she managed to become a chiropractor. That would have been a respectable way for her to make a living. Her pictures do not show her as a beauty, but she did marry again. This time it was to John Gable. We can only guess that he was in the lumbering business as they moved to Bemidji, Minnesota. It was there that Eliza Brant and Rowe McCamus met and married. Jennie and John Gable then moved to Lewiston, Idaho. This was also a logging area. Members of the McCamus family visited them there. There are pictures of Jennie's sister, Eva.

Jennie had her difficulties after she and her husband, John Gable, moved to Idaho. She began a millinery business. Somewhere along the line she had had to declare bankruptcy. An article in the *Bemidji Pioneer Newspaper* stated she had given her home to her daughter, Villettia. This property should have gone toward the payment of her debts.

It was in Lewiston where Jennie and John Gable both died.

ROWE MCCAMUS

I was terrified of my grandfather. Actually I think most of the family was afraid of him or at least intimidated by him. He was not a popular man with anyone. He had an irascible temperament. He was angry. He was disappointed with the world and his own life.

Rowe was born in Iron River, Michigan, in May of 1883. He was the first of two children born to Samuel McCamus and Elizabeth Rowe. His sister, May, was born two years later. The family moved to Toronto, Canada later. Rowe went to school in Toronto through the fifth grade. I don't know if he had further schooling or not. I know little about his early life.

He eventually ended up in Bemidji, Minnesota, where he met his future wife Eliza Brant. They were married January 28, 1905. My grandmother, Eliza, was sixteen at the time and probably pregnant if the date of the marriage is correct. My grandfather was in his early twenties. My father, Ronald, their first born, arrived September 2, 1906.

Before Ronald's arrival, Rowe and Eliza had moved to Brookston, Minnesota. They were probably assisted in the move by Rowe's father, Samuel. He owned some land there and had the McCamus savvy with money. Rowe began a newspaper, *The Brookston Herald.* He probably had had some newspaper training in Bemidji. He wrote clearly and carefully if in a somewhat stilted manner. Apparently the newspaper was successful as he was made vice president of a bank begun in Brookston and later he became president. Rowe was appointed postmaster in the small town, though Eliza actually did the daily work, and added to the family income.

Another child was born into the family, another male, Harry Clyde. He lived to be only three years old. Eliza and Harry Clyde both contracted diphtheria when an epidemic went through the area. Although Eliza survived Harry Clyde did not. A picture of a sweet three-year-old holding a kitten is the only surviving memory of the child. Tiny had his remains moved to the cemetery in Culver before she died. Both she and her husband Adolph are buried there also.

Three daughters were born to Eliza and Rowe. Elizabeth was first and ever to be known as Tiny because after the boys she was a tiny little girl. Then came Verona who was to have her life shortened by rheumatic fever. She died in her thirties. Marjorie was the youngest and perhaps most like her father.

It seemed a good life in Brookston despite the death of Harry Clyde. The family prospered and Tiny tells of her father, Rowe, giving her nickels to spend for candy. This good fortune was to disappear, however, when the raging Cloquet Fire destroyed the entire town of Brookston. Eventually some people returned although my grandparents did not. There is a small village there today. One of the few streets rebuilt is one named McCamus Street. This is our family's one claim to fame.

Rowe attempted to find work following the devastating fire. He went to Saxon, Wisconsin, to work in a bank. I don't know where the family stayed during this time. Rowe did not last long at the job. He returned to make an attempt at farming on some one hundred acres of land his father, Samuel, owned. Perhaps the family was already living on the farm after the fire. This venture did not work well either. The soil and climate were not conducive to growing crops and the livestock, probably sheep, did not prosper either.

Eventually, Eliza and Rowe moved to Duluth. They were both employed at St. Luke's Hospital, Rowe as a maintenance man and Eliza in the laundry. It was here that Eliza lost the third and fourth fingers of her left hand in the mangle.

Ronald, who was in his early teens, was living on a dairy farm at Barnum and working as a hired man doing chores and milking cows. He also attended Barnum High School. He managed this by rising early, completing his farm tasks, and riding a Greyhound bus to school. Meanwhile Tiny was attending school at Greenway High in Coleraine. She lived with a family named Gable, probably related to her grandmother's second husband. Education was the topmost priority for the family. The two younger girls, Verona and Marjorie remained in Duluth and attended school there.

I know of my grandfather only from the visits we had there in the summer when I was young. My grandparents lived just off London Road on 17th Street. The house had a porch on the second floor where we slept. My sister Barb and I were not allowed to go there because the condition of the porch made it unsafe. Being children we did not follow this rule completely and we would sneak on the porch to watch the multiple ore boats and other large ships approach the Canal Lift Bridge.

We were often taken down to the park to view the ships close up. This was our favorite pastime. Sometimes my grandfather, Rowe, would take us and sometimes my Aunt Marge would take us. I liked that best because she was more patient and we could stay longer.

My grandfather spent a great deal of time upstairs in the bedroom where his typewriter was located. He composed numerous letters to politicians and newspapers and sent them, I assume. I was horrified when I was studying at the University of Minnesota when one of his letters appeared in the Minneapolis Star. My grandfather was an arch Republican who often ranted against the Democratic administrations of Franklin Roosevelt and Harry Truman. This particular letter was written prior to the 1952 election. My grandfather wanted the Republican candidate to be Robert Alphonso Taft. Robert Taft was the son of William Howard Taft, the seventeenth president of the United States. He was a U. S. senator from the State of Ohio. He was the chief opponent of all of FDR's New Deal proposals. The candidate chosen to run for the Republicans was Dwight David Eisenhower. My grandfather, in his letter, designated Ike as a mugwump, that is, he had his mug on one side of the fence and his wump on the other. This was term which had been used in the election of 1832 when Republicans jumped to vote for Democrat, Grover Cleveland, because of the financial scandals surrounding the Republican candidate, James Blaine. The word mugwump is an Algonquian word meaning sanctimonious or aloof from the political process. My grandfather wanted a real Republican like Robert Taft. When one's last name is McCamus there was no doubt that the letter writer was a relative. Fortunately not many students read the newspaper then, either, and I escaped ridicule. There was a real contradiction in my grandfather's view as his son, Ronald, my father, was provided with a job when FDR expanded agricultural opportunities in the country.

My grandmother died in 1950. Everything changed then. It was already changing rapidly after the Second World War ended. I don't remember where my grandfather lived. I don't remember visiting the house after my grandmother died. I think we went to Duluth, but maybe we stayed with Tiny on the farm. This is hard to believe since she and Adolph had such a small house with only one bedroom. Perhaps Adolph and Tiny stayed with Adolph's parents who had a large house next door on the farm.

My Aunt Marge and my Uncle Tubby moved to West St. Paul. He had worked in Duluth for the Starns Architect firm. Then the son of the Starns entered the firm. My Uncle Tubby and the Starn son did not get along. Tubby, whose name was Harold Hanson, found a job at 3 M as an architect. This was a struggle for him, because he had worked himself up as an apprentice and did not have a university degree. However, he did well and traveled to Italy to build a plant after he had been with company awhile. Why my Aunt Marge did not go with him I'll never know. I think she believed that the United States was superior in every way to every country and she did not want to have to live in other cultural environments. But I didn't agree with my Aunt Marge's outlook on life.

I believe our family began to take other vacation trips about this time. There was gas. My dad loved to travel. Our first trip was to the Black Hills and Yellowstone Park. We had a tent and camped because we had no money. This was hilarious as I look back on it although at the time it must have produced some very frustrating tense moments.

I remember my grandfather did not like Harry Truman at all. Truman was somewhat of a hero to my father who considered him a man of the people and a defender of ordinary Americans. He spoke my dad's language and enacted policies with which he agreed. Once my dad received a large packet of articles my grandfather had collected from the newspapers all of them casting great insults at Harry Truman. Unlike my aunts who, while caring for my grandmother after her first stroke, vowed never to take care of my grandfather, my father said little about my grandfather. I think Marge started smoking after he died to spite him. I don't think she dared to defy his rants while he was still alive.

My grandfather did come and stay with us for a time when I was a teenager. He had a temporary job typesetting for *The Willmar Journal,* a weekly newspaper which was still being published in town. I don't know if the typesetter was ill and then came back or the paper went defunct about that time.

I was still afraid of my grandfather. My mother was teaching and busy as was my father. Maybe they were away. I don't remember the exact circumstances. Anyway I had to prepare a meal for him. I fixed a beef roast which was what he liked. I cooked potatoes and I even made gravy which was edible. This was a great hit to him. He praised me for it. Of course, I was one of only two grandchildren and I tried to behave around him because I feared his wrath so much.

Sometime after my Grandmother Eliza's death, my grandfather went back to his roots in Peterborough, Ontario, Canada. He visited the Minthornes, his aunt and uncle who lived in St. Catherine. He also visited his Uncle Tom, the most successful of the family, at least in a worldly way. Tom lived in New Liskerd, Ontario, in the northeastern corner of the province. He had made a great deal of money in the mining of copper and cobalt. He also owned a telephone line in New Liskerd. At ninety-three he had buried two wives and now had an attractive housekeeper, Mrs. Douglas. My grandfather was a self-centered man. He loved money a great deal. He hoped to be in line for some of Tom's money when he died. Tom had no children. However, Rowe also liked women and he became enamored with Mrs. Douglas. This was not at all popular with his Uncle Tom and Rowe was cut out of the will which was enacted after Tom's death. Rowe wrote an extensive letter to Tiny about this trip. This was how I managed to find Isobel McCamus Filmer after Tiny's death.

Rowe did not live a great deal longer himself. He died of a bowel obstruction in early September of 1953. He was not ill for a long period of time which was fortunate because of his daughters' refusal to care for him.

I have Rowe's DNA for better and for worse. I definitely have the political obsession and leanings although I am of the opposite persuasion as I am a left wing Democrat. Rowe was intelligent and determined. These are good qualities, I think. He married my grandmother and that was a good choice. He cared for his family and supported them. He strongly believed in education which is the best of his legacy to all of us. I always feared him although he was not unkind to me. Men at the time had to be fearsome perhaps. I am grateful for his inheritance despite my own raging anger at the world which is not too different from his. For better or for worse this was Rowe.

ELIZA BRANT MCCAMUS

I don't know a lot about my Grandmother Eliza's heritage. I do know that she was born in Jefferson township, Green County, Wisconsin. Her parents were Franklin Brant and Jennie Boyles. Brant is a German name and the original might have been Brandt. It is through the Brant side we are related to Bill Axt, my father's cousin who was a teacher in Superior, Wisconsin. Jennie's roots are Irish. Her grandfather was born in Ireland. The Boyles were very prominent around County Cork. Boyle is a common Irish name and so we may not be at all connected with the higher class Boyles.

I do know that Franklin Brant died of lead poisoning. He was a house painter and the paint at that time contained quantities of lead and was deadly. It is also true that in southern Wisconsin there are lead mines, and it is likely he worked in the nearby county in the lead mine.

Jennie and Franklin had three daughters, Velettia, Valeria, and Eliza. Jennie must have been a very intelligent resourceful woman. After Franklin died she moved about often. She educated herself as a chiropractor and so was able to make a good living for herself. She also remarried a man named John Gable.

The family lived in northern Minnesota some. Tiny mentioned they had lived in Bemidji and then Morehead. They moved finally to Lewiston, Idaho. That is where Jennie died.

Eliza met and married Rowe in Bemidji. She was only sixteen and when my father, Ronald was born she was only seventeen. She and Rowe moved to Brookston only to be wiped out by the Cloquet fire. They ended in Duluth in a house just off London Road on 17th Street. This was where we visited our grandparents when I was young.

Eliza was pretty as a young girl, but as she grew older she was a bit stout although her facial features were rather sharp. She had a quiet dignity about her that overcame what deficiencies she may have had in appearance. One took notice of her because of her intelligence and her elegant presence.

Eliza was not an affectionate effusive touchy person, but I always felt that she loved us greatly. She was a perfect housekeeper, not that they were well-to-do, but that everything was substantial and meticulously clean or well prepared. I particularly remember the white bedspreads that covered each of the beds on the three upstairs bedrooms. I scarcely dared sit on the bed because it was so pristine and smooth. We carefully folded it back before we climbed into bed at night.

I remember the old Victrola in the dining room where I listened to the old Harry Lauder recording of "Tip Toe Through the Tulips" and played it over and over again.

My grandmother was a superlative cook. I would go to the fruit and vegetable market with her and she would pick the sweetest cantaloupe available and the freshest green beans. We had very formal dinners where the table was set with her best dishes and silverware and with glass goblets on a perfect white linen tablecloth. We had candles on the table, too. No wonder my mother was intimidated by her in-laws coming as she had from the subsistence farm in the woods. My grandmother served dinners of roast beef, mashed potatoes, green beans or squash and a pretty gelatin salad. We had homemade cake and ice cream for dessert. I loved the meals she fixed. She made beautiful jams and jellies which could have won prizes at the State Fair.

Best of all, my grandmother took us to all my favorite places. We would take the bus to downtown Duluth and shopped at the Glass Block and Gold something stores. Then we would go to Bridgeman's for an ice cream soda or a sundae. Sometimes she would take us to a movie. This was a special treat. She always bought candy at the Fanny Farmer Store. Since my mother was particular about what we ate we had limited amounts of candy at home and never the good chocolates.

On a pleasant day we would drive up the North Shore for a picnic on the rocks on the shore of Lake Superior. We would have fried chicken and homemade potato salad and brown sugar cookies. It was a spectacular setting and the fresh air made food even more delicious. My grandmother, however, was very fussy about where we climbed on the rocks. She was safety conscious and our freedom was somewhat restricted.

I think I was most affected by who my grandmother was. She didn't talk a lot, but what she said was very apropos and her intelligence would shine through her conversation. I loved her.

I was seventeen when she died of a stroke on January 13, 1950. She wasn't terribly old. I don't think she was sixty. That's the only time I remember my dad crying. He didn't sob, he just sat quietly as the tears dripped down his cheeks. I can still see him sitting on the crouch silently grieving.

CONFLAGRATION

This is the story my father told to me, my much loved, thoughtful, almost always ill Daddy. It is this story he told that I wish to tell. It is not this time the story of my daddy himself which someday I shall find the courage to write.

The little town was called Brookston. It's still there, not really large enough now to even be called a village. It has a street named after us, McCamus Avenue, our only claim to fame. My grandfather and my grandmother were very young when they came there, and they were very busy in this place in which they wished to fulfill their dreams. I think my grandfather only went through the fifth grade in school in Toronto where he had lived as a child. Yet he had his own newspaper, *The Brookston Herald*. He was so prosperous, something I find difficult to believe, that he also was an officer in a bank. The reason I find it hard to believe is that we have never been prosperous. Of course, we always had enough to eat and a place to sleep and we even had our teeth fixed. But rich and prosperous bankers we were not.

In addition to caring for my father, my Aunt Tiny and my Aunt Verona, my grandmother was the post mistress. My Aunt Marjorie was yet to be born. My Aunt Tiny was not tiny. She once said she was called that by my grandfather because she was the first girl after the two boys were born and she, by comparison, was dainty and female. She wasn't large, but she definitely wasn't Tiny when I knew her. My father had had a brother Harry Clyde. I have his photo when he was a sweet three year old, and he is holding a kitten. His grave is beside the grave of my Aunt Tiny. He died in a diphtheria epidemic in the early twentieth century. Tiny lived until 1994.

But this is a different story, too, than that. It occurred at a desperate time in history. It was a dark black moment in a world which had many dark black moments. I'm thinking it happened in 1917, but the written accounts say it was 1918. Memory is not always a reliable factual tool. I hope it is more reliable in an emotional way. It's not the way things actually came to pass, but that it satisfies me to remember it that way. And memory is a precious part of each of us. We have to remain skeptical, of course. I have always smiled at the statement I read somewhere long ago. "The world as you remember it, never existed."

But I continue with diversion instead of telling the story my father told.

It was October, one of those beautiful hot days, when everyone thinks summer may return in spite of the gold and crimson leaves on the trees and the laggard rising sun. It was not unusual to smell smoke in the air in the autumn in the thick woods that surrounded the not quite Village of Brookston. I think I forgot to tell you that both the St. Louis River and the Great Northern Railroad ran through Brookston. The trains carried iron ore, timber, passengers, and general freight supplies. The train was important for the commerce of Brookston which had a population of about five hundred people. It did have promise, this small burg. The railroad is crucial to this story.

Fires were common in the fall in this northern country. Settlers burned land to be cleared for farming. They burned the residue of their crops. The loggers were required to burn the slash left from cutting the trees so as not to leave fuel for a larger fire. But by far the most fires were caused by the railroads. Live embers from the coal fired engines spewed forth in spite of laws that had been enacted to equip each locomotive with spark arrestors and safe fireboxes. Minnesota law even required that the railroads send patrols along the tracks during fire season to check for fires and to extinguish them.

It had been a hot dry summer followed by a hot dry autumn. In this hot dry October smoke was often in the air. It was ordinary and commonplace and usually taken as part of living in Northern Minnesota. My father was thirteen that year. My Aunt Marjorie was not yet born. There were just my grandfather, my grandmother, my father, my Aunt Tiny, and my Aunt Verona who later died at thirty of rheumatic fever.

Yes, it had been a hot dry summer followed by a hot dry autumn in a period when there had been many hot dry summers followed by hot dry autumns. But on this October day a cool northwest wind quickly changed the temperature and brought relief from the heat. There was always a smoke in the air in the autumn, but this was different.

This day, October 12, 1918, was somehow very different. That's what my daddy said when he told me about it. There had been fires burning for a day. They had begun about five miles away from Brookston at Mile Post 62 on the south bank of the St. Louis River. This was the place where logs and poles were loaded on the trains. The area surrounding it was covered with wood chips and shavings ready for the sparks from the train.

The smoke became increasingly thicker and more penetrating. The air was heavy and the brisk wind could not blow away the smoke. The sun was red in the sky through the smoky atmosphere and the winds were increasing in velocity. The smoke became more and more dense and excluded the sun and closed in and locked the town in a deep dark penetrating cloud. I am trying to imagine this, but not too much, because I am terrified of fire.

Now my grandfather even with his ambitions and dreams and the fact that he was my grandfather was not a pleasant man. He was an angry irascible man who did not get along well with anyone. (My mother used to tell me when I was at my worst that I was just like my grandfather. That was not a compliment. But I was a difficult child before I became this difficult adult.) That again is another tale. If my grandfather was not a nice man, he was not a stupid man. He was Scots-Irish with all the knowledge that the world will sooner or later break your heart and he knew that the promises of this day were not the promises of light and hope and fulfilled dreams.

Now my grandfather was not the only up and coming resident of Brookston. In fact he was not the most outstanding citizen. He did not own a car. But the most prominent member of the community was the proud owner of a brand new Model T Ford. This was significant and perhaps there is a moral involved if I were Aesop telling this story that my father told me. Or perhaps the lesson is Biblical instead.

As the smoke gusted in with the wind and became more and more oppressive, my grandfather knew that this was a day of consequence. He and my grandmother talked to neighbors, and scanned the sky, and talked to each other. My grandmother and my grandfather then quickly decided that they must leave. This fire was not like all the other fires. They could sense it in the smoke filled air and it became increasingly difficult to breathe.

They pulled some of their possessions out of the house. I don't really know what they had that was valuable. Perhaps they had some papers and some pictures, some books, some heirlooms. I don't know. The bank had a vault and they placed a few meager possessions in the vault. Many people buried their most cherished possessions and never were able to locate them after the fire because all the landmarks were gone.

There was a relief train stationed in Brookston, a freight train. My grandfather and grandmother had decided to climb on that train with their family and leave their town, their home, their possessions, and perhaps their dreams behind them. They had to evacuate. There was no choice. My grandmother packed suitcases and lunches and took whatever food they could carry and they walked to the train depot and waited with two hundred other residents of Brookston. As they walked to the station, their neighbors drove by with their new Model T heading out of town to the safety of Cloquet.

The short train was quickly filling and the family squeezed into the freight cars, pushed together like cattle. The doors were kept open there in the thick smoky air which made breathing increasingly difficult.

The train was crowded, overflowing with refugees from the quickly spreading terror, this enemy this looming monster called fire which took no prisoners and gave no forgiveness. I picture the train with the passengers, the old and the young sitting squashed together in the cars and the men and women standing sideways stuffed in, falling out the openings and the doors and the train streaming through the smoke and darkness and foreboding speeding away from the fire.

The train chugged and the people of Brookston and the surrounding villages gasped and choked in the crowded cars some with handkerchiefs in front of their noses and some just were just struggling to breathe. The children cried and the old people had tears and looks of confusion and dismay upon their faces.

The fire was being fought back so the train could leave Brookston. With shovels and water the brave men struggled to clear the tracks for the train. They did not know that one mile down the line where the train and river turned south at Flint Pit the fire raged. When the train reached Flint Pit there was no choice. The train continued through the flames and smoke and some of the passengers on the flat cars were burned by the heat and debris as they went forward. In a miracle the train passed through the worst of it and into a clear place and on to Cloquet which had not yet been threatened by the fire.

My grandfather jumped off the train, leaving my grandmother, my dad, and his daughters still aboard. He looked about him sniffed the air, and talked to some of the people on the platform. He again boarded the train. "We are not getting off", he told them. "This train is going on to Duluth and we are staying on it. We are not getting off here in Cloquet. This is no ordinary fire. We are going as far away from it as we are able to go."

My grandfather had made a wise decision. It was not many hours later that the fire engulfed Cloquet and its residents fled into the St. Louis River to escape with their lives. Shortly the train resumed its route and it was chugging to Duluth. There was a little more room now, but it was still crowded and there were still crying children and downcast older people and anxious and fearful adults in the car.

The smoke was everywhere and although it was lessened somewhat when they arrived in Duluth it was still in the air. Later it was learned that winds had climbed to 65 miles per hour with gusts in the 80's. The relative humidity is perhaps the most predictable sign of how dangerous a fire may be. That day the relative humidity reached the lowest reading that had ever been registered in Duluth, 21 per cent.

At long last, the train pulled into the station at Duluth and the crowded cars dislodged their passengers. Then there was a scream. The children clutched their parents in terror. There was yet another horror to be faced. The massive flu epidemic which added to this black and catastrophic time of World War I had not yet abated and the employees in the train depot were wearing gas masks to ward off the plague that was killing thousands of people in a world which it seemed God had forgotten.

My grandparents never really recovered from the fire. My great grandfather, Samuel McCamus had a little money and bought them some land outside of Brookston. The land was not productive and my grandfather was not much of a farmer and this did not work out.

My grandparents eventually moved to Duluth where they worked at St. Luke's Hospital, my grandfather as a custodian and my grandmother in the laundry. My grandfather also had jobs setting type for newspapers throughout the state later in his life. He lived with us for a time while he worked for a local Willmar weekly paper.

However, the people with the new Model T Ford did not make it out of the fire. The whole family perished driving through the forest. What would Aesop's moral be? What would be the Biblical lesson?

Many of the people who disembarked in Cloquet had to walk into the St. Louis River to escape from the flames, but some people also perished. Although less famous in Minnesota history than the earlier Hinkley fire, the Cloquet fire destroyed more acres of forest and killed more people.

My grandfather suffered from destroyed dreams, but he and my grandmother had escaped with their lives and with their children. I am grateful of that for otherwise I would not be here to tell the story my daddy told to me.

Perhaps this also explains the mystery of my father's pessimistic declaration when events seemed to be turning in the wrong direction and misfortune seemed to be closing in on us. He would say ironically, "Cheer up the worst is yet to come." Pollyanna he was not.

THE YEAR WAS 1933

I never knew her. I never knew anything about her. I didn't know the story until I was almost sixty years old. Even then it did not arouse my imagination and my emotions until after my Aunt Tiny died five years later. I was the executrix of Tiny's estate as the only relative around. Even then I think she would have chosen someone else if she hadn't liked my husband Don so well.

Great Aunt May (right) with her friend Rose. (left)

Tiny had never been a particularly good house keeper. After all she had been a childless elementary school principal. She was preoccupied with her job, the church, and with spurring my Uncle Adolph to behave. She was good at giving orders. She was not well organized, however. This seems to be a trait I share. She had not been well those last couple of years either. It was my job to go through and inventory her possessions. I wouldn't have minded the clutter, the messiness, but her house out there in the woods of St. Louis

County west of Cloquet was infested with kangaroo mice. I went through the years of accumulation which included some family heirlooms and some very interesting old stuff. Nothing was very valuable, but to me it resonated of memories and questions. I didn't mind the main floor too much as I was sorting and sorting and sorting I managed to set aside the family belongings from those items which were to be included in an estate sale. It was the basement that got to me. There was an old day bed down there which was completely mouse infested. There were boxes and boxes of clothing and documents. There was my grandfather's hat, the one I remember him wearing to Willmar to see us. There were hats of my grandmother's too. There was a band uniform about which I had no idea at all. We ended up taking it to the Cloquet Museum. I have made this sound organized. Actually it was strewn all over the floor. There were letters and pictures and papers thrown all about. I don't why or how this happened. But my curiosity was greater than my revulsion. My gag reflex worked well I discovered, but I had to know what was there. I gingerly picked up these mouse chewed paper remnants and took them home with me. I know they should have been burned and I probably contracted some terrible disease from them, but I took them home. I am still relatively well and have no sign of mouse borne disease. I told no one for a long time, because my hygienic friends and relatives may have stopped socializing with me entirely. I am very grateful that I picked up the papers and took them with me. I'm also glad I have no symptoms of a rare disease. In these papers I found letters from my grandfather to my Aunt Tiny.

The most revealing letter was of the trip he had taken to Peterborough, Ontario, Canada where the family had settled after their departure from Ireland. This was the notoriously hilarious trip he had taken from Peterborough to New Liskerd, Ontario. Here was where his ninety something year old uncle who was a mining engineer lived. Uncle Tom was reportedly very rich. He owned cobalt and copper mines and had started the telephone company in the small town where he lived. My grandfather liked money a lot. I think his intention was to make certain he had a designated spot in the old man's will. My grandmother had died a few years before this trip. Uncle Tom had a very attractive housekeeper of about sixty or so. My grandfather who had more than one vice was immediately captivated by her. This was obvious to the old uncle who although old still had his mental faculties. To say that he was not happy would underrate the situation considerably. My grandfather returned home without the housekeeper and without being named in the will. I hesitate to think how rich we could have been.

My true inheritance was the mention of Peterborough. Family members had always said there were no more McCamuses. When your name is McCamus and you have searched phone directories all over the United States and some places in Canada, you believe this to be true. With my terrible curiosity I had to go to Peterborough. There I found McCamuses. They aren't on our branch of the family, but I did find a relative with a family tree and lots and lots of information. I still don't know any relatives in our line of the family although I have tried to contact a number of people who might be related. Probably most of them aren't, but some may not have wished to acknowledge any blood relationship.

In my Aunt Tiny's mouse chewed papers I found other letters. One of the letters was written July 6, 1933. It begins:

"Dear Elizabeth,

Do you need a new dress and do mine fit you well enough to buy a new one I just had made and have worn only five times?...I am so blamed hard up and no job in view that I would like to sell the dress if possible."

This letter was written by my Great Aunt May. She was what was once known as a maiden lady. She had never married. She worked in a department store in Spokane when the depression hit. She describes the dress in detail to my Aunt Tiny. She is concerned that she has lost so much weight that her two remaining dresses, one silk for summer and one wool for winter, will no longer fit her. She goes on to talk about her job situation. She says:

"Right now when so many just out of school are looking for work and many willing to work during vacation for almost nothing, there does not seem to be many jobs for anyone as smell as I." I think she meant small because that side of the family had many short slender members. It is an interesting kind of Freudian slip about her self-worth.

I then found a letter written November 15, 1933. It was a letter carefully typewritten by my father to my Aunt Tiny.

"Dear Tiny,

I don't believe I would worry about the accident itself or the way Dad acted about it. You know he takes most things rather queerly, so I should expect him to take this in the same way. He was surely wrong in not answering the telegram because he was keeping the Walla Walla folks in suspense.

I never dreamed that she was in such hard circumstances although I suppose I could have suspected it. But I don't think that could have been her reason entirely because she could have gotten some place where she was not in want. Perhaps you never knew as much about her as I did. The grandparents had some very odd ideas as you can probably judge from some of Dad's. I don't think she had a chance to do things as she would have like as a girl. Likely some of the plans or many of the plans she had made were spoiled. Looking back on those things and thinking she was all alone and the depression on top of it I suppose she didn't feel that life was worthwhile. It could have come without any hardships to contend with. So I would try not to think of it if I were you."

My father went on to a different subject. Again I quote:

"Anne and Beverly Joan came home last nite and both are feeling very fine...I found plenty of excitement in the first real nite being a father, as I got up and brot Baby Beverly in for her midnite lunches. But it will go fine when we get into the routine of things."

I knew nothing of my Great Aunt May for many years. I didn't really become interested in the family history until long after my dad died in 1971. In fact I did not become interested until my Aunt Marge died in 1990. There was only Tiny left then. She was my only living source of information. I asked her many questions about my great-grandparents. She talked some about my grandmother's parents and siblings. She said almost nothing about the McCamus family, except Uncle Tom who was so successful in a worldly way. She answered none of the questions I asked about my grandfather's mother except that she was English. Her last name was Rowe and my grandfather had inherited her irascible bombastic temperament as well as his first name from her. I believe there are two different great-grandmothers on that side of my family. What happened to my grandfather's mother? I asked about her mental health and her death and lots of other questions. Tiny refused to answer. It is my belief that she ended in a mental hospital or whatever they had where ever she was in Canada or in the state of Washington. This is only a guess.

Tiny did talk about Aunt May a bit. I think she still felt guilty about not buying the dress.

The accident my father euphemistically referred to in his letter to Tiny was my Great Aunt May's suicide. She could find no work and she was in despair. Conservatives say that people did not jump off buildings and commit suicide during the Great Depression. It's just a distorted liberal myth according to them. My Great Aunt May jumped off the department store roof to the street below and committed suicide. I have her death certificate somewhere. I have the McCamus DNA and I'm not organized at all, but I continue to search for it. Someday I'll find it in the boxes and totes and files of papers and pictures and documents. She fractured her skull when she landed from her fall. Today they would say she died of traumatic brain injury.

I have not found her death certificate, but I did find two pictures of her. She seems very happy in them. She was young then. She looks like us. She is small like my aunts and dark haired and wears glasses as we did. She is alone. I also have a box I found at my Aunt Marge's condo which contains a partial dresser set. The box is labeled Aunt Mae's ivory dresser set. She died in 1933. My Aunt Marge misspelled her name writing it Mae instead of May. She didn't know the date of her death. The set was not ivory either. My Aunt Marge was always pretty self-absorbed and she didn't pay much attention. So this is my inheritance from May McCamus. I have a letter, two pictures, and a powder box and a rouge box and wonderful comb. I also have her near sightedness, her wordiness, and her tendency for depression. We share the DNA. We share that spiritual inadequacy that reveals itself in our loneliness, our pessimism and our hopelessness. I fight it every day. God love us all.

VERONA, MARGE AND TINY

TINY

My Aunt Tiny was not really Tiny. She wasn't huge either. She was in between. Her nickname didn't make much sense really. I asked her how she came to be called Tiny. She was third born in the McCamus family. My father, Ronald, was the oldest. Next came Harry Clyde, who tragically died of diphtheria when he was only three. All I know of him is the picture of the sweet little boy hugging a kitten to his cheek. Next was Tiny. She was a girl, a tiny thing compared to her brothers. Thus my grandfather always called her Tiny. How it stuck all those years until she died at 84 I don't know.

My first memory of my Aunt Tiny was when I was nine. I had bravely taken the train from Willmar to Duluth to stay with my grandparents and my Aunt Tiny. She picked me up in Duluth and took me out to the farm west of Cloquet where she and her husband Adolph lived. They lived in the same farmyard with Adolph's family, the Johnsons. Adolph's older brother Oren still lived with his parents. He was one of the Norwegian bachelor farmers. The Johnsons had carved the dairy farm out of the woods. They milked cows, raised potatoes for the Duluth schools, and also had some small grain and corn which was used for silage.

I loved that farm. I rode Tiny's bicycle up and down the gravel road, went to the Culver store for groceries and helped Tiny can sweet corn at the community canning facility which had been set up in the county for the use of residents. We picked blueberries and in her yard we picked sweet peas and nasturtiums. We washed the separator which was used to separate the cream from the milk. I learned how butter was made by mistake. I had the task of whipping cream and I was so industrious it turned to butter. We took the buttermilk to Mr. Johnson who was mowing the lawn and found it a great treat. I could not understand this as I thought it tasted terrible, but I was glad that my mistake was not a disaster.

The best time of all was when I accompanied my Uncle Adolph out to the pasture to bring in the cows to be milked. Their beautiful collie dog, Shep, came with us. Adolph teased me all the way. It remains a delightful memory. Milking the cows was fun. The kittens in the barn ran all about waiting for the squirt of milk which Oren placed right in their mouth.

Adolph and Oren seldom left the farm except to play horseshoes or attend the Proctor Fair. Both of them liked to drink beer and apparently it was available at the fair.

Tiny went everywhere in the United States. I think maybe she didn't get to Alaska, but by the end of her life she had been to all the rest of the states.

As the years passed, we made yearly trips to Duluth and to the farm. Then my grandparents died and my Aunt Marge and her husband moved from Duluth to West St. Paul. After Tub died Marge moved to Sun City, Arizona. My Aunt Verona had died of rheumatic fever sadly before my grandparents. We continued to make our yearly summer trips west of Cloquet, near Culver, to the Johnson farm. This was a yearly ritual until all of them were dead.

My most vivid and precise memories of Tiny were in her later years. Although quite feminine in lots of ways, she had always been an outdoors person. She loved winter which was a good thing, living where she did so far north. She cross country skied into her eighties. She stayed on the farm until winter was almost over. Then in April she went to Arizona.

My Aunt Tiny was an elementary school teacher. She had managed to go to high school by staying with some friends in Coleraine. Then she attended teacher's college in Duluth. She taught in a number of schools in St. Louis County. Eventually she completed her degree in elementary Education in the 60's and then became the principal of the Alborn School. She taught for over fifty years. By the time she retired she had had three generations of students from the same families. This did not occur because she was a gentle, tolerant, kind, diplomatic person. She possessed none of these qualities. She told everyone exactly what she thought and that was that. Just before she died a third generation student came to visit her in the hospital. The young woman had a baby and was not married. Tiny began the conversation with, "I don't suppose you're married yet. When are you going to do that?"

Tiny was a member of small rural Lutheran Church about two miles from the farm. She contributed generously and worked hard particularly during the summer to keep the church going. She, however, was appalled that the pastor wore plaid flannel shirts to the church and she told him so. She pretty much ran the church and I'm certain although she left a nice legacy when she died that they really missed at least her money.

Tiny's biggest hang up was hair. She herself had a short haircut which was naturally wavy. The hair style fit her well. When her hair became very gray she colored it a darker gray and sometimes it turned blue from rinse. When my hair became very white, she suggested I do the same. Since I am as stubborn as she is and have the same gene pool, this never occurred. The most amusing thing she said about my hair, however, concerned the length of my hair when Don and I were married. She said in her blunt way, "You know your hair was too long when you got married." This came out of nowhere, so I was surprised as Don and I were approaching our fortieth wedding anniversary. I could only laugh. I said, "Yes, but the marriage lasted anyway."

I once visited Tiny in Sun City, Arizona, at the condo which my Aunt Marge had purchased there and Tiny had inherited upon her death. We had gone out to eat at the cafeteria. My Aunt Tiny loved cafeterias. We sat down at a table. Then a young man with red hair and the largest red beard I have ever seen sat down at the next table. My Aunt Tiny covered her face with her hands and said loudly, "Isn't that terrible!" She was referring to all the hair. We changed tables.

My Uncle Adolph was bald and this may have been the reason Tiny married him. No hair. When he died his grandnephews were his pall bearers. One of them had just received his PHD in mathematics and was on his way to a position at the University of Washington. He was a nice looking young man and was attired in a white shirt and a good looking sports jacket. The problem for Tiny was that he had shoulder length hair. It was shiny and clean and would have been the envy of many females. Tiny approached his grandmother. There was no conversation about his accomplishments, about his destination, about his marital status. No, the assault was on Tiny's obsession. "If he were my grandson, I'd cut off that hair." Having known Tiny for almost sixty years, Adolph's sister, Cora, only smiled.

My Aunt Tiny was usually only direct, out-spoken, and opinionated. She was angry when my Aunt Marge died. Marge was the youngest in the family and eight years younger than Tiny. Tiny was outraged that Marge had died first. That was not the way it was supposed to be. Tiny was older and should have died first. She was furious about this until the time when she herself died.

I miss her.

MY AUNT MARGE

Why is it only now that she is dead that I can begin to feel compassion and try to understand her? Why did I resent her so while she was alive? She didn't really ever do anything to hurt me. She expressed her opinions that was all. It was my fault that I didn't like them. She was honest. I can't blame her for not being honest.

She did separate herself from us, of course. She did remove herself. But was that because of wanting to remove herself or did we, too, distance ourselves?

I didn't understand her. Not at all. I heard what she said. I saw what she did or didn't do, but what was behind it all?

She was the most intelligent of all of us, I always thought. She was the prettiest of all of us, too, when she was young. And she was the wittiest and the most fun. Yet she didn't really do anything with all her gifts. That was part of the reason I resented her. She didn't try to do anything with it. Why wasn't she more curious about things? Why didn't she ask more questions? Why did she just fit in? But she didn't always fit in. She smoked all the time wherever and whether anyone cared or not. She was very independent and stubborn and defiant. She seemed like she was still rebelling against my grandfather's wishes with the smoking. He hated smoking passionately and relentlessly. Yet she smoked continually. She was a chain smoker.

She was the youngest in the family, a lot younger than Verona and Tiny, my dad's other sisters. And she must have been fourteen years younger than my father. And she was such a cute child and so precocious. Everyone loved her and spoiled her. She used to run up to my dad and give him such a big kiss and hug. She was very affectionate. I remember the story they would tell about being in the woods picking blueberries, when an old Indian came up with some candy and said, "Candy for the papoose."

I don't know much about her growing up, but very late I learned that she was sent to live with my mother and dad just after they were married. She had gotten into some trouble, shoplifting or something. She had bad friends and my grandmother couldn't handle her. It would be a certain thing that my grandfather couldn't. He was not tolerant of human weakness and mistakes, and expected always that his idea of right and wrong would be followed. My mother never talked about it, but she always must have resented it, for it came up so late and so vigorously when she finally told me about it.

Marge was young when she married. She was only nineteen, I think. I was the flower girl. She was a beautiful bride. She married Harold Hanson Jr., her Prince Charming and built her whole life around him. And he was a catch. He was tall and handsome and intelligent. He worked as an apprentice to an architect named Starn in Duluth. He was conscientious and capable and learned well. Why he didn't go to college, I don't know. He and Marge were both very independent. They had little money in those days. They didn't own a car, but then this was the late 30's and the country was still in a depression. Lots of people didn't have cars. They lived in a duplex up the hill from my grandparents in Duluth. I remember one of our family stories. We had come from Willmar to visit. Barb was a preschooler. Marge had made a tuna hot dish, again showing the McCamus thriftiness. When she removed the cover from the casserole, the aroma of the food permeated the house. "Phew, whose feet stink!" Barb exclaimed . Our Mother was mortified although the remark was ignored by everyone else. Mother didn't want to hurt Marge's feelings. I think also that she was a little afraid of Marge. There must have been sixteen years difference in age, so I don't understand that at all. Why was Mother so intimidated by her?

Marge moved back to my grandparents' home when Tubby, her husband, was drafted into the service in WWII. She lived with her parents and took piano lessons and became a fairly good pianist. Tubby was stationed in New Guinea. He was in the army I believe. Nothing much was said about his army experiences, ever. Whether he ever saw military action in the Pacific, I don't know. I believe he worked with the army engineers. When he came home he went back to the architectural firm that Starn had, and Marge quit her job at Montgomery Ward.

Marge and Tub didn't have any children. They seemed to like children. Marge treated Barb and me so well when we visited. She and Grandma took us to the zoo and shopping and always to the harbor to see the ships. There was always special candy and ice cream at Bridgemans and walks and rides on the merry-go-round.

I don't know how she felt about not having children. I don't know if she wanted children and couldn't have them or if she didn't really care. She was the child in the marriage. She played and catered to Tub. Perhaps it was because she received no positive attention from my grandfather. She probably helped make decisions and arrange their social life, but the real responsibilities of making a living were his.

When Starn's son entered the architectural firm, Tubby found they were incompatible and so he began looking around for another job. He had taken college courses by this time and had good experience in both building residences and in building businesses on the range and also in Northern Michigan. Since he was so well qualified, he was hired by 3M even without a degree. Marge and Tub moved to West St. Paul. Tub must have made a very good salary, since they lived in a beautiful area which had a woodsy location on the edge of the development. Wild life visited them. They would see deer and fox and had wonderful birds at their bird feeder, rose breasted grosbeaks and cardinals joined the nuthatches and the chickadees.

They belonged to an exclusive country club and Marge played a lot or golf and bridge. Tub travelled to Italy for 3 M and other places in Europe to supervise the building of facilities . Marge never went along. She didn't like to travel. I think she found Europe inferior to the United States and she did not want to go there and be less comfortable than she was at home. How could she not want to see that art and history?

She, like my grandfather, was a rock ribbed Republican, Conservative to the core. She worked for Governor LeVander after she and Tub moved to West St. Paul. All her views were strong and followed her own inclinations. No one else's opinion mattered.

Things went well until Tub had his heart attack. They were already making plans for retirement. They had been to Arkansas and Arizona. They had decided they liked the planned idea of Del Webb and Sun City, Arizona. Marge wanted him to quit, although he had been with 3 M for only ten years. Tub wanted to complete his degree in architecture because the younger members of the staff were paid more money than he was even though they did not have his knowledge or his experience. He also wanted a bit more money so his pension would be larger. 3M was pressuring him to return to work. He went back and sat at his desk and had another attack, this time fatal.

I remember going to the home of her friend who lived in the same West St. Paul area after Tub's funeral for lunch. The friend was kind to serve the food, but in a discussion I overheard her say, "I always found the Bible to be very boring. I never could read it." The superficiality of the life Marge had seemed never more apparent.

Marge sold the house and moved to an apartment. This is

one time she indicated that she was unhappy. She soon decided she was going to follow their retirement plan and move to Sun City. She was only 55 at the time. She said she hoped she would be happier there.

We never visited her in Sun City. We saw her at Tiny's in Culver in the summer when she came to visit and she came to Willmar to see my mother. She always gave an open invitation to come and see her in Arizona, but we had the children and we had no money. When we took a vacation we went to see other people. I just didn't understand her and we certainly did not agree on much.

It was only several years after her death that I visited the condo. It was very like her. It had a lot of DeGrazia prints on the wall, cute little girls. Everything was tasteful, kind of small like Marge. There were lots of tiny cutsy figurines. Tiny said she kept the condo very dark. The blinds were always pulled.

She had little to do with people who were her neighbors in the condo association where she lived. She would play golf with her friends, play bridge, and go out to eat with them. In fact, she ate two meals a day in the restaurant. She didn't want to eat alone although she did a lot when she ate out. She never cooked. She read newspapers and magazines and watched TV, I suppose. She had money, at least enough, although I thought perhaps she might roll that into a fortune, but she didn't. And, of course, she smoked. It was as if her only true friend was a cigarette. She would fill an ash tray at breakfast and continue on all day at the same rate.

Mother would say how sad Marge's life was, but I don't think I ever understood. She must not have wanted to go back after her visit with Tiny on the farm west of Cloquet the last time. She went to bed and she did not get up. She died a few days before she was to return to Sun City.

I look at the old photographs of her when she was growing up and she always looks so unhappy. She is sullen and unsmiling like the world has played a great trick on her. She stands rigidly and stoically as if she can scarcely bear and endure her life.

In the condo I found a dresser set belonging to unfortunate May, my grandfather's sister who committed suicide when she lost her job during the depression. There were also Christmas cards and letters from Marge's friends. She sent a lot of them and received a lot of them in return. She had carefully annotated notes on the outside of the envelopes about the state of the friend's health or the problems they had or the losses that they had undergone. I'm of mixed emotions about this. It was so methodically done in such a business like way. I have just a few friends and this seems cold to me somehow, yet I sometimes in my self-centeredness forget what is happening to my friends' lives. I always wonder why she was not close to anyone, not even to Tiny.

I wonder why they sometimes called her Jereke? Marjoreke, I guess.

I think of Emily Dickensons' poem "The Soul Selects Its Own Society" when I think of Marge. When Tubby died, she seemed to close the door. She was very lonely and really didn't have much of a life for herself. She saved her money and left it all to us, but really did not give of herself, but shut herself away. I don't understand.

I inherited her condo with Tiny's death. I visited Tiny once in Sun City. We went out to eat with a friend of Marge's. Both Marge and her friend bragged that they had read the whole

Bible. Then Marge's friend said she was leaving the church she attended because they had let in all those alien Mexicans.

I don't think Tiny could bear to sell the condo because of Marge. This was depressing to me. I feel I have the whole family on my shoulders. I am carrying them around with all their memories and mine combined. It's only me left and I have the children, the progeny, the only future beyond this generation.

The life in Sun City was Marge's American Dream. They had by middle class standards made it. Here was the ideal managed retirement community. Here was the anytime golf, the social life, the absence of responsibility. It was their dream and I think it was empty for her, but I don't know if she thought the emptiness was because Tubby was not there or because she realized the dream itself was flawed.

It seems ironic that this dream I find so barren is by chance incorporated into my life. There must be a reason for it, some meaning I am to acquire from it. Funny, I always find meaning. But then my problem has never finding meaning, it is finding too much meaning to comprehend.

MY AUNT VERONA

I don't remember my Aunt Verona very well. She was born between Tiny and Marge. She had very dark hair. In her pictures it looks black, but it may have been just a very dark brown. She also had fair flawless skin. She was thin, unlike the rest of the family.

She graduated from high school in Duluth probably. She worked after she graduated. I don't know where, but it was probably a retail job. I don't know if she moved to Minneapolis to work. I thought this was a possibility, because she married Allan Ford on September 8, 1941. I think she was older than he was by a year or two. He was born in Minneapolis and lived there.

My other aunts talked of Verona as somewhat of an adventurer. She was not conventional and she liked to play and have fun. I don't know when or where she contracted rhematic fever. The disease did serious damage to her heart.

She was not the lucky one in the family. Soon after she and Allan Ford were married, World War II began. I don't know if he was drafted or if he enlisted. He must have had some education since he attained the rank of Major. I never met him.

My Aunt Verona, because of her illness, was unable to work and she lived with my grandparents while Allan was in the service. I didn't see much of her because she spent most of her time in her room when I was there.

She did travel to Virginia for a time to be with her husband. I don't know if she had to return to Duluth because of her illness or if he was deployed to Europe.

She came to visit us once in Willmar. I don't remember her well from that visit either.

I have a small box of letters which were written to her by Allan after their marriage. I also have several large framed pictures of her. She was an adult and perhaps the picture was taken just before she died.

My aunts used to say I had hair like Verona's and skin like Verona's. My skin is certainly not flawless and I just don't know about the hair.

Anyway, the concern was that Allan would die in the war,

killed in battle. In great irony, it was in fact Verona who died from her damaged heart.

I would have liked to have known her.

DADDY

Ronald Rowe McCamus was born September 2, 1906 at Brookston, Minnesota to a seventeen year old mother and a twenty year old father. His middle name came from his father, Rowe, who in turn carried it as the family name of his mother, Elizabeth Rowe.

There is a baby picture of him, but the picture which I carry in my memory is of a young boy of about ten or eleven looking anxious and tense and a little afraid. At that time his father was publishing a newspaper in Brookston and Rowe also had a position in the town's bank. This I find very surprising as a lack of money was a constant in the family for as long as I can remember. Eliza McCamus, Ronald's mother, my grandmother, was the post-mistress in Brookston.

This Is Who We Are

Ronald had a just younger brother, Harry Clyde who died of the diphtheria that struck him and my grandmother. She miraculously recovered. He did not.

Following Harry, the three daughters were born, Elizabeth, Verona, and Marjorie. The family evacuated Brookston as the Cloquet Fire devastated the whole area. Not so famous but much larger in scope than the notorious Hinckley fire, it wiped out the dreams of the family. Ronald wrote an account of the fire for the *Willmar Tribune* much later. I'm confused about Marge's existence at the time of the fire. I don't know if she had been born then or not.

After the fire the family moved to a farm in Western St. Louis County which had been purchased by Rowe's father, Samuel McCamus. But Rowe was not a farmer and the acreage was not farm land. They survived, but Rowe moved from the family to Wisconsin to work in a bank. This was not a satisfactory arrangement either, so eventually they moved into Duluth where Rowe became a maintenance person at St. Luke's Hospital and Eliza worked in the laundry. Rowe later worked as a typesetter for various papers and owned a popcorn wagon in Leif Erickson Park along Lake Superior.

Ronald was the oldest and the only male child in the family. Fortunately the arrogant McCamus family was proud of its brains. They also believed in education. Thus while on their farm, Ronald went to live with a dairy farmer at Barnum. Clem Hanson was a farmer in the area who was known at the time for his innovative and careful farming practices. Ronald rose early in the morning and assisted with the milking. He then took a Greyhound bus into Barnum where he attended high school and eventually graduated.

Then somehow, Ronald managed to go to the University of Minnesota. It is easy to imagine him sleeping in the barns while he worked on the farm owned and run by the University. This probably isn't true, but he did work and he did manage to go to college. There is a copy of *The Gopher* of Twenty-seven, his annual. In his picture there, he is much more gaunt and thin than in his later photographs. Still there is the anxiety, the tension, and almost fear in his eyes. He had graduated with a degree in agriculture and was prepared to become a county agricultural agent.

His trajectory following graduation is a bit unclear. There was mention of MacIntosh, and Grand Rapids. He was eventually hired as the county agricultural agent for Koochiching County and lived in Baudette. It was in Baudette that he met and married Anna Smith who taught fifth grade there.

It was the Great Depression. There were not funds in the impoverished Koochiching County to retain a county agricultural agent. Ronald and Anna and half of the Smith family retreated to the subsistence farm the Smiths kept at Gemmell, half way to nowhere. They could eat there, sleep there, and work there. It is difficult to imagine Ronald helping Anna's brothers cut pulp wood, but he and they were not strangers to hard work.

Then a break came for Ronald and Anna. FDR and the New Deal brought in new programs for agriculture and some money. He had an opportunity to go to Kandiyohi County,

Willmar. They moved to an Eagle Lake cottage. By that time their first daughter was on the way. They moved into town.

The first memory I have of my father was before I went to kindergarten. He always walked to work and home again when he wasn't making farm visits. It was winter. Perhaps I was four. I was outside in the yard of the house we shared with an older couple who lived upstairs. There was snow and I was making snow angels and waiting for Daddy to come home. When I saw him on the sidewalk down the block I ran to meet him. He grabbed my hand and we walked home.

When I was sick with a cold or flu, he would come into my room after he came home from work. He would read the funnies to me or perhaps a library book. Then he would stay with me and his paper. If one image remains with me of my daddy it is of him reading the paper. There are pictures of him with me and my sister reading his paper. There are pictures of him with my children reading his paper.

Sometimes my dad would take me with him on farm visits. Very often I would go on 4-H tours in the summer. We would go from farm to farm to view the 4-H members' projects. He would kindly discuss the animals and the showing abilities of the members, offering gentle suggestions about caring for the animals and showing them well.

Once I even had an opportunity to go with him to the St. Paul Campus at the University of Minnesota where he met with some colleagues. It must have been during WWII as we took the Greyhound bus. He did not drive in our '39 Ford.

Daddy was good with people. He was also knowledgeable. Whenever I needed the answer to a question I went to him. He squeezed my hand. He called me Bevie. No one else called me Bevie.

My daddy couldn't fix anything with his hands. I can recall my mother's tirades about things that needed fixing and they were never fixed unless she fixed them herself. This would not have been quite so bad had we had the money to hire someone to fix things, but we didn't. At least I don't think we had the money. Daddy was very tight. He was always after us to close the doors and turn off the lights. We ate well, but new dresses were a rarity. Snow boots and school shoes were purchased, but there were no Sunday shoes. Daddy and my mother, who was used to having her own money, often had spats about expenses and how to keep them down.

My mother was of strong German descent, a school teacher who was a tough disciplinarian. My sister and I disagree about whether our mother threatened us with the hair brush and razor strop or rather she used them. I only remember the feelings of shame and terror. I don't know if she employed them or not.

Daddy, on the other hand, never lifted a finger. I don't remember if he spoke a harsh word. I only remember the feelings of shame and terror he invoked when he shook his head in "no" or he looked dismally disappointed at something I had done. He was a gentle man.

Daddy was known as Mac throughout the county. My grandmother, Eliza, was also known as Mac, but not my grandfather, Rowe. Rowe was bad tempered, erratic, and angry and people avoided him, if possible. He lost a number of printing jobs because of his impossible temperament. Daddy took after my grandmother, I guess.

Mac seemingly knew everyone in the county. People would stop and talk with him wherever we went. At the time, I thought that every child was treated as well by people as I was, but I know that I received innumerable passes on my behavior because I was Mac's daughter. It was a favoritism that few others received.

I don't know if the illnesses my daddy had were because of the weak constitutions of the McCamus family or if it was hard work and endeavoring to please everyone that took its toll. Perhaps it was some of both. In the spring Daddy would have terrible bouts of poison ivy. At that time they sometimes put him in the hospital. He also had stomach ulcers and once again he would be hospitalized.

During WW II he was not drafted. He had a job that was considered valuable to the war effort. He did not receive raises, however, and he was not highly paid. Because of this, and because labor was in such short supply, he took on a second job. Willmar was a railroad hub at that time. Cars of fruits and vegetables passed through the town. These cars were cooled by blocks of ice which were placed by hand. This is the job my daddy took. He was exhausted much of the time, but it was WW II and he was not alone.

After the war he dropped the second job, but continued nonstop with his ever expanding role as county agricultural agent. When I was a sophomore in high school, he suffered a severe heart attack. Fortunately he survived. It changed him though. He would walk home at noon for lunch and take a nap. They placed an assistant county agent in the office to help him. Home agents were beginning to appear during this time as well. These arrangements sometimes worked well and sometimes they didn't, human personalities being what they are. Daddy did, however, try to rest more and please a bit less.

Daddy's sense of humor was visible most of the time. My mother was strong-minded and difficult. He would handle her in the most clever ways. One of the ongoing disputes they had was over the temperature in the house. Daddy liked it cool. Mother liked it hot. He used to say to my religious mother, "Annie, you will never go to that hot place, hell. You would be too comfortable."

After I was married and the county agents were better paid, my parents were able to purchase a bigger house. I actually had never lived in a house they owned. It was always a rented house. This was partly because we could not afford to buy and partly because my mother could never find a house of which she approved. Finally they bought a house on Southwest Sixth Street. In this last house in which they lived, there was space and comfort. It was Christmas time and my mother was baking. This increased the already high temperature in the house. My daddy was in the den writing

Christmas cards. My mother walked in the den to talk to him. He was stark naked. It was his statement about the temperature. My startled mother laughed and told the story often. I doubt if it changed her mind about the temperature she liked, however.

My daughters remember their grandpa taking them to the park when we visited them in Willmar. They loved it, because they could do whatever they liked to do with no interference. Grandpa had brought his newspaper and was reading under a tree. I don't recall any serious accidents while he was with them. He had a calming influence even on my wild farm raised daughters. They were safe.

My father lived until he was 65. He had not retired although he had plans to do so and write some after he did. He was in the hospital with the endocarditis which took his life. We were visiting him. My young daughters were not allowed in the hospital at that time of strict rules. They stood outside his window. The medication he had been taking had destroyed his ability to hear. We used our own sign language and wrote notes. He had perked up considerably as he managed to get to the window to see the girls. I wrote a note to him in his room. "The girls think you look good, Grandpa". He said with his innate sense of humor, "Oh, that's what all the girls say." And that is the last I remember him saying.

I learned a few things about my father after he died. One farmer complained bitterly about the bad cigars he smoked. I had forgotten the cigars. He quit smoking them after he had the heart attack. I also learned he was a shrewd poker player. In later years he went to the country club on poker nights. He couldn't drink because of his recurring ulcers or at least he couldn't consume much alcohol. Perhaps that's the reason he won so often. He had, or course, a wonderful way of reading people which had to be helpful when he was playing poker.

The most interesting thing of all that I found out about my daddy was his connection with the country and the time in which he lived. On a trip I took to China, I was flying in an airplane with other members of a tour. In the seat next to me was a fellow who was in the New York State Health Department. He had once been a county agricultural agent in New York State. I told him of my father. He said, "Most of those old guys were loved and respected. They were a part of Roosevelt's New Deal programs. The farmers were so desperate and he gave them hope and the ability to make a living. The country agents were the recipients of that gratitude." I had thought my daddy was just a good guy. I hadn't thought of his connections with something larger. What a wonderful revelation!

At my 55th class reunion, a classmate of mine, mentioned something about amiable. I didn't hear his whole sentence. Since I was back in Willmar, I thought he was talking about my daddy. He said, "Oh, him, too. I meant you." Whatever amiability he found in me was from my daddy.

Of all the good fortunes in my life and I have been a very fortunate person, none other is greater than the good fortune I had in having the best daddy anyone could ever have.

MOTHER

Anna Myrtle Smith McCamus, my mother. She was born at Mikado, Michigan on January 15, 1904 to Anna Grimm and George Henry Smith. Anna was the fourth of seven living children, following Ethel, Edith and George Gustav. After Anna came Carl and the twins, Rupert and Ruth. My cousin Ann Bruder told me that the oldest child my grandparents had died in infancy. Her name was Helen. That would make my mother the fifth born.

Anna was red haired, lively, mischievous and strong-willed. She was her father's favorite, and she returned the favor by never saying a disparaging word about him. As far as I know from my mother, my Grandfather Smith was a candidate for sainthood.

I know of this early period only from my mother and the stories the family told about her. The only event she told about Mikado was running barefoot over the slats in a bridge and stepping on a snake sunning itself in space between the boards. This to me is a metaphor for our family. My mother did not think in that way, in spite of her religious beliefs. It would not have occurred to her to make this link with Adam and Eve and the human condition. It was simply a terrifying incident which remained with her for her entire life.

Smith Family at the farm in Gemmell, MN
Back row: Anna, George & Ethel
Middle row:: Carl, George, Edith &Anna
Front Row: Twins Ruth & Rupert

The family moved many times while the children were growing up. My grandfather farmed, worked as a carpenter, and labored at logging camps. They lived in Michigan, Wisconsin, and North Dakota. In Wisconsin they lived for a time with my Grandmother's mother Regina Rusch. I blamed this roaming on my grandfather's Native American heritage. His mother was one quarter Native American and part of the Brothertown Nation in Wisconsin. However, when I mentioned this casually to a woman who was almost my mother's age who knew a great deal of history and of the customs of the time, she said this was common during the period. Men were looking for work which was scarce. Perhaps both things are true and more that I don't know about. Life is complicated and there is no one reason that answers every question.

The family finally settled in Gemmell, Minnesota, which was then a small thriving lumber town. Gemmell is between Bemidji and International Falls and about as remote as any place could be in Minnesota. It was here my mother grew up. I remember the farm. Who knows how correctly I remember, but I have mental pictures of the tar paper two story house, the log building where ice was stored under saw dust year around, and the built in the hill shelter for the two cows who furnished milk and butter for the household.

There were multiple relatives who joined the family at the farm at various times. Both my grandmother and grandfather had step-brothers and step-sisters as well as their own siblings who stayed and worked with them. My grandfather was a foreman on a logging crew for a time. Grandma cooked at the logging camp off and on as she could.

One of the stories my mother tells is of the acting troop of which she was a member. Always trying to make money for survival, the group which included my Aunt Ethel, my great Uncle Bill Rusch and my mother travelled around doing melodramas. My mother was a tall eleven at the time and played the maid in the play. This did not last long as it turned out to be a money losing venture rather than bringing in any extra funds.

It was a subsistence life they led much of the time. They had abundant wild game and my Uncle Carl hunted from the time he could hold a gun. Often he went out at night with Indians who lived in the area. This frightened my mother and my grandmother.

The family picked milk pails full of wild strawberries, raspberries and blueberries which were canned and preserved. The family had a large garden with root vegetables and short season crops. These were stored in the root cellar which was always a dark scary place to me. I would go down with Grandma for supplies, and I imagined a lot of stories about it. Sometimes Grandma had to bargain with the grocer for staples which they did not have like flour and sugar. There was a small income from the oats and flax they raised on the cleared land.

I sometimes think I can taste my Grandma's homemade bread with the freshly churned butter and her wonderful jam. I have never had anything like it since she moved from the farm when I was very young.

The family burned wood which they had cut. Some of this was for the wood cook stove. The chimney caught fire one winter. They managed to put it out, but Mother remembers the snow filtering in through the hole in the roof which remained until the weather was suitable for it to be repaired. Mother claims she woke up in the morning with a small drift of snow or her blankets and quilts. No wonder she was always cold.

Gemmell had a high school with some good teachers. Ethel, George, Carl, and Ruth and Rupert, and my mother all attended high school and graduated. My Aunt Edith had a severe disease in her childhood. It is my memory that Edith and my mother both had Scarlet Fever. My mother recovered with no serious complications. My Aunt Edith suffered brain damage from the high fever which racked her body. My cousin says that Edith had encephalitis and this caused her difficulties. It is among the things I will never know. It was not talked about much and I only remember Edith helping my Grandmother, sweeping the floor and washing dishes. Edith went to school for a while, but eventually dropped out because of her impaired abilities. She eventually was placed in an institution in Cambridge.

I don't know much about the teachers in Gemmell. I do know that my mother and my Uncle George bragged about getting 100 per cent on their State Board Algebra Exam. The whole family could quote reams of poetry from memory. They recited from Tennyson, Wordsworth and the Romantic English poets as well as Edgar Guest and James Whitcomb Riley. My mother loved Riley's "Little Orphan Annie" and gave us large quotations from it. Perhaps it was because she also was sometimes called Annie.

They seemed to have a lot fun when they were young in spite of the hardships. It was common at the time to promote a lot of box socials and home grown parties which usually took place at the school. My mother, as I have already stated, was somewhat of a scamp. One time Mother and her cousin, Elsie Reinarz, attended a pie social at the school. The man who owned the logging camp, whose name was Leon Hoyt brought his new car, a Model T Ford to the social. It was parked in front of the school. Mother had never driven a car, but she and Elsie decided to take it for a ride. She and Elsie drove to Mispah on dirt roads. On the way back she hit a large rock and broke the axle. Her brother Carl was furious with her for doing such an impetuous thing and being so destructive. Leon Hoyt apparently forgave all.

Another time, the community had a pie social and Mother made a pie and took it to the school to be auctioned off. She and Elsie had concocted a plan. It was a mud pie she and Elsie made and disguised as the real thing. Again the unsuspecting Leon Hoyt purchased it and discovered the hoax. My mother was a charmer I guess. My grandparents didn't lose their jobs. Maybe they were that accomplished at their tasks. When asked my mother's reply to her shenanigans was simply, "Gemmell was a very boring town. I had to do something to liven it up."

The funniest story I didn't learn until my cousin told me about it recently. Mother's cousin, Dewey Miller, was staying with my grandparents on the farm. He had a wonderful and very cultivated handlebar mustache of which he was very proud. One day he decided to take a nap on the day bed in the living room. My mother hit upon the hilarious idea of attacking his mustache while he was in deep sleep. She took the scissors and neatly severed it on both sides, trimming it back considerably. The consequences of this prank I do not know. I find it very funny at this point of my life. The mother I knew was not at all prone to these actions. She was very proper. Perhaps that was why she was so strict with Barb and me. She outguessed all our maneuverings outside acceptable behavior.

The family would often travel many miles to a dance on Saturday night. They would take a railroad car and pump it sometimes twelve or fifteen miles. They would wear their old shoes to tromp to and from the railroad and tie their good shoes around their necks so they could put them on when they arrived at the dance hall. They would dance late and long and sometimes sleep wherever they could and return home in the morning.

Mother was just seventeen when she graduated from high school and decided to go to Normal School for the summer to become a teacher. She borrowed $90.00 from my Uncle Carl who had been in Ellendale, North Dakota, helping harvest potatoes and actually earned some cash. Bemidiji had just opened its teacher's college. They did not have a building for an assembly meeting, so they put up a large tent. Unfortunately, they situated it in a bed of poison ivy, and many students had bad cases of it after meeting there.

Mother's first teaching job was at Craigville. She earned $85.00 a month. There she lived with a trapper and his wife. As Mother remembered them, he had long hair and a beard. His wife was as wide as she was tall. Mother stayed in the same room as their mentally handicapped daughter. In winter a fire had to be started in the school before the students arrived. Mother talked about hearing the wolves howl as she made that early morning in the dark trek to the school. The trapper's son followed her to school with gun in hand to protect her. One morning as she walking she felt something flick past her leg. It was a shot from the gun. She walked on as if nothing had happened. When she finally looked back at Floyd, the trapper's son, he was as white as the snow that surrounded them.

There was a beaver hanging outside the window of the bedroom where Mother slept. It was winter and the beaver was frozen solid. One day it disappeared. The meat she had for supper the next day was unusual. "Oh, no I'm eating beaver!" For as much wild game as the family had eaten, she had not eaten beaver before.

My mother went on to teach at Hackensack and Pine Island. Then when she couldn't find a teaching job, she worked at Dayton's in Minneapolis in the fabric department. After that she found a teaching position in Baudette. It was there at the boarding house where she ate she met the young struggling County Agricultural Agent, Ron McCamus. They married and then she entered her period as Ann or sometimes Anne with an e on the end.

She much enjoyed being Mac's wife with all its privileges and she played on it for years even after he died. She lived on for another twenty years without him. She was 87 and begging to die when she passed on.

Nana Ostrum on left holding Bobby, Me sitting and Grandma Smith on the right.

MY LITTLE SISTER BARB

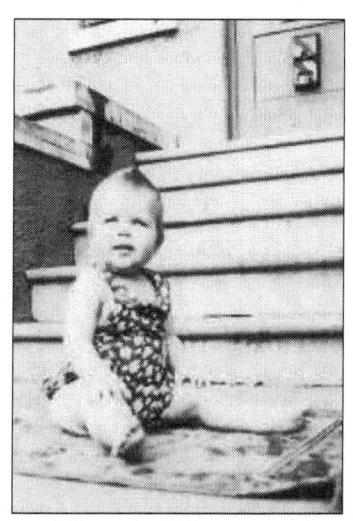

I was almost four years old when she was born, October 7, 1937. Once when she cried for a long period of time I asked my mother if we couldn't send her back. She had some difficulties eating when she was young. She probably had some food allergies which were not diagnosed back in the thirties. She looked and seemed very healthy, however, except for some problems with eczema.

Always strong minded, I remember her going outside barefoot when she was about four and walking in the newly tarred street in front of our house. My mother was livid and talked about it often in following years.

She was always a good student and teachers liked her a lot. When she was in sixth grade she started an elementary school newspaper called *The Little Willie*. My mother wanted us to have every advantage and so we both took piano lessons. I began with Mrs. Wahlstrand, our neighbor. Then my mother heard that the nuns at the convent across town were excellent piano teachers. This meant that we had to walk about two miles across town to the convent on the West side of Willmar. We lived on the East side. Barb and I disagreed about my mother's slant on practice, but then she was always more disciplined than I was. I remember my mother sitting with the yardstick on the piano bench making certain I put in my one hour a day practice time. I think occasionally she used it, but Barb doesn't remember this at all. We'll never know who was right about the happening.

Barb eventually performed at a piano concert all by herself. She was that committed. I never was and always struggled with activities I would rather do. Neither of us was terrifically musical anyway.

I think Barb was president of her class. I can't find her annual so I don't know if I remember correctly.

Barb graduated from Willmar High School in May of 1955. Then she went on to the University of Minnesota. I think originally she planned to be a doctor, but changed her mind somewhere along the way. She was, again, an exceptional student. Accepted to a SPAN trip to what was then the Union of South Africa, she wrote a paper on the labor unions there as a means to equality of the races.

Barb went Connecticut College for a year. She was the maid of honor at Don's and my wedding in December. She took a Greyhound bus home a few days before Christmas. She had to change buses in New York City and missed her bus to Minneapolis. She had her red velveteen bride's maid dress in her luggage which was lost. Even more serious she left her notes from her SPAN trip on the bus also. I had bridesmaids from several places so I had purchased the red velveteen material and sent it with a pattern to my sisters and my friends in the wedding. Red is not easy to match, but my ever- suffering father took us to Minneapolis to purchase red velveteen fabric which, by a miracle, was identical to the red of the other dresses. A woman down the street who was a seamstress sewed on Christmas Day and finished the dress. The next day Barb's suitcase arrived with the original dress. This was the irony of ironies.

The following year Barb transferred back to the University of Minnesota. She graduated in 1960 a member of Phi Beta Kappa and with a Woodrow Wilson Scholarship to Johns Hopkins University in Baltimore. She began her graduate studies the following year and this is where she met John Conder. They taught with a different and more symbolic literature system there. It was also barely the end of the fifties and there were few opportunities for women who were expected to marry and not to work and especially not to have a career. Milton Eisenhower, the brother of Dwight D. Eisenhower the President of the United States, was the President of Johns Hopkins. My father wrote him a letter about sex discrimination. Not much happened. Barb transferred to the University of Wisconsin at Madison and back to the Midwest and a more understandable English program. She received her PHD from there and was offered a position at Carlton College in Northfield which she accepted.

In the meantime John Conder had accepted a position at the University of Wisconsin. They dated and during this time purchased the Andy Warhol print of Marilyn Monroe. There is some confusion as to whether Barb or John bought it, but an item in the Minneapolis Star attributed it to Barb. It now belongs to John's niece, Dan's daughter who is in an art field.

Barb and John decided to marry and so Barb left her prestigious job at Carleton and accepted a position at Janesville in the University of Wisconsin system. This was the Vietnam War era. John was teaching in Madison which was one of the hotbeds of anti-war activity. In an incident there, a bomb was set off which resulted in the death of a science researcher and injuries to others. John and Barb decided to head south where there was less violent activity. John had been offered a position at Vanderbilt University in Nashville, Tennessee, and they moved there. Eventually they purchased the house on Bresslyn Road. Barb began teaching night classes at a branch of the University of Tennessee. She loved this teaching because the students were largely adults who wished to better themselves with a degree and greater writing skills. They were ideal students.

There always seems to be turmoil around the academic community. The faculty was required to publish works in their field and there was a lot of competition among the faculty. John eventually became a full professor and survived the politics of the school. He was always very independent and did not follow the leader of the department well and so there was much anxiety in the household.

Barb did not fare as well. A segregation suit resulted in the mingling of the state of Tennessee system which was almost entirely black with the University of Tennessee system which was largely white. This turned her schedule upside down. She was teaching early morning classes at Tennessee State and evening classes at the University system in downtown Nashville. She simply couldn't handle the routine and could not find a way to change it. She resigned and became a pickup professor at Vanderbilt. She did not make very much money and she was teaching writing which meant she was correcting many, many essays, not an easy task. She did this for a number of years. She also completed a book based on her thesis on Thomas Hardy. The timing was bad for this and it was not accepted by the publishers. She couldn't seem to get a break.

We saw each other occasionally. We visited them sometimes on vacation. Barb would have dinner parties with friends who were faculty members. She bought country ham which was smoked and was a special treat. John and Don drank a lot. Don managed to get along well with John and everyone else as he always did. My memory dwells most on the visit when the girls were young and John had just bought a beautiful glass paper weight. It was passed among us and Nancy dropped it on a glass coffee table. Their house was not child proof. Nancy was always the careful one of our daughters and we were shocked when this happened. We had no money to replace their expensive furniture and I still feel guilty about it.

I always thought John and Barb believed they were above us. One Christmas when I was feeling particularly humiliated I sent John the gift of a bottle opener in the shape of a jackass. This far outweighs the paper weight incident as it was a mean deliberate act.

Barb and John always had a dog. Most of them were Doberman Pinchers and they were well bred and cost a lot of money. This dog is very intelligent and loyal and they were also known to be good guard dogs. They had a series of these dogs most of whom did not live a long time. Once I remember them hiring a dog psychologist because the dog would not descend the steps that led to the outside. Neither Barb nor John would force the dog and often it had to be carried down the long flight of stairs to the back yard. I think the psychologist told them just to make the dog go down, but this did not work well. The trait remained until the dog died.

Barb and John visited Willmar when our mother was alive. One year they came for Christmas and the weather was colder and snowier than it had been for years. Barb and John were staying at the Holiday Inn across town. Don had to transport them in the subzero weather with wind blowing snow everywhere.

John always chose and gave special gifts. They were beautifully wrapped and delighted all the recipients especially my mother who seemed to worship John. In the last months of her life when my mother was in the nursing home, she had a stroke. She could no longer speak and make sense and her right side was paralyzed. This was in December just before Christmas. She waited I am certain for John and Barb to arrive. They had final grades to process before they could leave. They spent an afternoon with her. That night she had another stroke. She did not have a Living Will but she had wanted very much to die for at least the last two years. We did not try to extend her life, but let her pass on. She had seen Barb and John and all of our family and she was ready to go.

Things did not improve for Barb. John was killed in a car accident going to work. He hit a tree in their older car which did not have seat belts. He murmured something about a buzzing sound when the medics arrived. He was taken to the hospital but his aorta had been injured and he did not survive the surgery. We do not know whether the buzzing sound was a bee or perhaps a brain aneurism or a stroke.

Barb continued on in the beginning, teaching some writing classes. Tennessee was changing however and she had some very rich conservative students in class. Their parents disputed grades and the students refused to read some assignments they felt were too liberal. She decided not to do this any longer. She did assist some grad students in the writing of their dissertations. She saw some of their old friends, but they began moving away and dying. She kept the Doberman they had had and she adopted a rescue dog. Joey was a Springer spaniel and had an off kilter eye. He was very obedient and sweet tempered. Barb kept him until he died. She did not replace him.

She did make a trip to a Russian Orthodox monastery above the Arctic Circle in Siberia. It was led by a professor from

Vanderbilt and she loved this trip. She also came to see us in Winnebago and I travelled to Nashville to see her.

Barb planned a trip to Spain with an old friend who lived in Pennsylvania. She had to fly alone to the country and had an anxiety attack which landed her in the hospital. She was unable to go and really did not travel after that.

She began to have more difficulties with depression and probably with alcoholism. She became a hoarder. The last times I went to see her I spent a great deal of time ridding her of newspapers, periodicals, and junk mail. Some of her bills were not paid. She had cataract surgery and she had had a detached retina on the one eye. It required a high priced specialist to remove the cataract. Medicare would not allow him to do the other eye and she could not figure how to solve this problem. She could read only by shutting one eye and tilting her head. Eilene and I went to see her and helped her go to her doctor and schedule the cataract surgery on her good eye. We also set her up with a new therapist as her other therapist had retired. We thought we had helped with things, but she resented us and had little to do even with me after this visit.

Barb became very reclusive. She did not interact much with anyone. Most of her friends had moved away or died. Her neighbors tried to engage her, but she did little but say hello. Even Bob True, who was her financial advisor and also with his wife a good friend, could not arouse a response to his requests. She had money and checks which were not cashed. She no longer drove, but had a taxi cab which took her after dog food when Joey was alive and also brought her food. The Appalachian mother and daughter who cleaned her house also ran errands for her, buying wine, I think. I don't know how Doris and Cindy cleaned but they washed the dirty dishes and scrubbed the bathrooms some. They needed the money and she paid them well.

She refused to see me at all. I wrote to her and she returned the letter saying she would not open any mail from me or answer any phone calls or come to the door if I were there. With Bob True's help I tried to get help for her. She was always very articulate and there was no way she would agree to be helped in any way. No health or social worker would evaluate her as vulnerable at least not in Tennessee. She would allow no one in the house which had become a disaster, full of trash and it was dirty and unlivable.

I had thought when Joey died the situation would change for the worse. It did. I did not know that he had died until a neighbor told me after Barb herself had died.

I only knew of Barb's death when the neighbor across the street called me early one morning and expressed her sympathy. Apparently Doris and Cindy had come to the door and she did not answer. They called the authorities who investigated and found her dead. Mike Varichak, my son-in-law, tried to contact the police in Nashville, but they would only talk to the Fridley Police Department.

Kathy, Eilene, Nancy and I went immediately to Nashville. We eventually received the information about where the body was held. We arranged for memorial service at a funeral chapel which Bob True had recommended. The police came to the chapel to take a sample of my DNA so the body could be released. We planned a short service which Bob True as an elder in the Catholic Church performed. Since Barb's old will had left a lot of money to Vanderbilt, Eilene contacted them to make certain some representative from the English Department came to the service. We shared stories of Barb.

We had to return to Minnesota before Barb's body was released. Eilene and I returned later in the year to bury her ashes next to John's. Bob True accompanied us.

Barb and I took such different paths. She worked so hard all her life with few rewards for her efforts. She did not have religious beliefs although there were books about Jesus and Christianity throughout her house. Life did not treat her well. I think I was too heavy-handed. She said I had hurt her greatly and she did not want anything more to do with me at the end. I have regrets, but she did choose her own way and I could not reach her. God bless her and keep her!

TREPIDATION

I regarded the trip with trepidation and dread along with with anxiety. I had to return to Nashville to claim my sister's ashes and to bury them.

It had been only after three police officers arrived at the funeral home to place a swab in my mouth and obtain a sample of my DNA to prove that I was indeed Barbara's sister that the medical examiner would release her body. Since my daughters' time was limited and we had allotted only a week for her funeral arrangements, Barb's remains were not present at her memorial service. We returned to Minnesota before her cremated remains were sent to the funeral home. Thus it was that I had to return to Nashville for this final task.

My sister, Barbara, died in February. We had hoped her brother-in-law, Dan Conder and his wife Patsy would be able to travel from Vermont during the summer to attend the brief burial service. They wanted to make a sort of pilgrimage in honor of Barb and John. This was not to be. Patsy had had many lung problems over the years. I was only vaguely aware of them from what Barb had told me. Patsy had a bout with pneumonia in the spring and summer. She was ill once again. Also Dan and Patsy were expecting a grandchild and were needed to assist their daughter after the birth.

I had only met Dan twice. The first time was at John and Barb's wedding in Willmar. He was thirteen years younger than John and in his early twenties when they were married. He had little to do with me or my husband Don at the time although he was the best man and I was the matron of honor. The second time I saw him was at my brother-in-law, John's funeral. By that time he was married to Patsy. I'm not certain I remember correctly but I think that was his second marriage. We did talk a lot at that time, but I do not remember much about it.

Dan was a Social Worker, retired now. He did not have the intensity that John and his sister, Eileen, both projected which almost overwhelmed anyone in the vicinity of their presence. Patsy was very chatty and seemed quite ordinary in contrast with the Conders. I liked her very much on first meeting.

The Conders lived in Linden, New Jersey, a suburb of New York City, actually. That our very rural family should be matched with such urban sophistication was difficult for me. My husband, the farmer, handled it much better than I did. Of course, he always handled everything much more easily than I did.

John's funeral had taken place at a large Russian Orthodox Cathedral in downtown Nashville. John's mother's ancestors were Russian. They were Catholic, but Russian Orthodox. I was fortunate to be aware of this church. I had never known anyone else who belonged to it. I grew up in Willmar and at that time I thought the only denomination was Lutheran, even though I was raised as a Methodist. John did not attend church. As I recall, however, he was extremely interested in the Cistercian monasteries in England, when we visited him and Barb there. John had an exchange teaching position in Leeds in the late 1980's.

The interesting part of the funeral was what I learned about

John's family. I had always felt great inferiority to Barb and John, mostly because of their intelligence and education, but also because I felt we were hicks in comparison to their urbaneness. John's sister Eileen and my daughter, Eilene, who shared the same name, also shared the same directness and bluntness and the attitude that the truth is most important. Let the chips fall where they may. Eileen Conder told the story of her grandmother whose husband died young. She had been left with John's mother and three other daughters to raise. She became the housekeeper of the priest, I assume Russian Orthodox. Eileen implied that this relationship may have been an intimate one although no more children were born to their grandmother. Money had been inherited from the priest and his family.

John, Eileen, and Dan's father had been a labor leader at General Motors for years. There was money in the Conder family and Eileen and Dan talked of the bar that was owned by their father's father. They stayed open during prohibition and they expressed some speculation about boot-legging. The stories put them almost on a level with our family.

I had hoped once again to see Dan and Patsy, but it was not to be. They were unable to make the trip to Nashville. My two Minnesota daughters were unable to accompany me either. Kathy did not have the money after her husband's almost two years of unemployment. Nancy was deep into a kitchen remodeling project and exploring colleges for Nicole to attend next year after her high school graduation. She also had a demanding job which she did not feel she could leave again. I know she works for the government, but she is very conscientious and very capable no matter what is said about government employees.

So it was up to Eilene and me, that is, my daughter, Eilene, who lives in Liberty, Missouri.

I had to be at the airport early in the morning. The plane was leaving at 8:15 a.m. Usually my daughter takes me downtown to catch the light rail, the Hiawatha, to the airport. This is easiest for everyone concerned. This morning was Labor Day, however, and I was a bit worried about the schedule and making it on time. My son-in-law offered to take me all the way to the airport. I needed the company and it relieved my time anxiety somewhat.

I easily met my Eilene in Nashville at the Enterprise rental car counter. We checked in to a Residence Inn and purchased some lilies to place on the grave site where my sister's ashes were to be buried. We went out for dinner at a local barbeque place. The barbeque in Nashville is as good as it is in Kansas City near where Eilene lives. I also had my favorite fried okra which is only available in the South and almost redeems the South from my deep prejudice against Southern States. Fried okra and Southern writers have made my life richer.

The next morning we drove to Calvary Cemetery where we met sweet Billie Orange, the young mortician from the funeral home. Bob True, Barb's financial advisor, who is now retired and works full time as a Deacon of the Catholic Church, arrived soon after we did. Billie was concerned about the wasps which were circling about in the grass. They were, however, respectful and did not disturb us. Billie had also brought beautiful pink roses to place on the cask of ashes and on the grave. Barb was to be buried next to her husband John in the gravesite they had purchased some time ago. Bob read some scripture and some Catholic burial prayers. Then Billie and an assistant placed the small cask in the prepared site. We placed flowers upon it. They then covered it with the pile of soil and replaced the grass over it. We laid our remaining flowers on top of the grass.

That was when Bob True told us this story of his parents. His mother was ill and died. His father was devastated and continued to grieve. He was very lonely and could not recover from his loss. He committed suicide. Bob found this extremely difficult to reconcile. One day he decided to visit his parents' side-by-side graves. As he was there, a dove flew down to Mother's grave and landed and then a dove flew down to his Father's grave. Then they both flew off together. Bob said that then he understood.

We then felt that my dear sister was now with her husband and this was how she wanted it to be. At last she was at rest and we could be reconciled to her death.

This should be the end of the story, but my trip back to Coon Rapids was remarkable. After all my apprehension, I found all of the two days an inspiring adventure.

Eilene and I parted company at the Nashville airport. I had so much to think about and everything had gone so well that I was calm and hopeful. I didn't even worry just a lot when the plane which was to take me to Chicago's O'Hare for the first leg of my trip was late arriving at the gate from which we were to depart. I did, however, go to the desk at the gate after a very kind Canadian woman who was trying to return to Calgary, Alberta, told me we would have to take a shuttle to another terminal at O'Hare. She told me about her last experience trying to return home from Nashville. She had had to spend two nights in two different airports because connections were not made. It was a nightmare.

I went to the desk and told the clerk that I was afraid I would not make my connection. I don't move very fast and the time would be tight. He informed me that another flight to Minneapolis would leave one hour later and he could offer me a seat on that flight. I would have a seat on both flights. If I made the first it would be fine. If I did not, I could fly out on the following flight.

I deboarded at O'Hare still not knowing whether I could make my reserved flight or not. The kind lady from Calgary quickly asked the desk clerk where to catch the shuttle. Then she asked me how fast I could walk. She would show me the way. I said, "Walk as fast as you can. I will try to keep up."

We came to the shuttle station. There was a long line. I wondered if we could all get on. Somehow we did all crowd into the bus after what seemed an intolerable wait. We hopped out. My gate was one direction and hers the other. I arrived at mine just as the plane was leaving and so I inquired about the next flight to Minneapolis. I hoped the woman from Calgary had made her connection which was twenty minutes later than mine.

I bought myself a hamburger as it was dinner time. The only food available on that end of the airport was McDonald's. I didn't want to risk missing another plane so I gladly ate the burger.

As I stood awaiting boarding time on the plane, I felt pressure on my leg. I looked down and there was a small boy of Indian origin from India. I had talked to him earlier and now he grasped my leg and kissed it and kissed it. His mother came over and told me he greatly missed his grandmother and he was attracted to anyone who reminded him of her. I was not the right color, but I did have the white hair.

This is not the end of my airline adventure. I sat next to a man who was returning to Minnesota to work on a high voltage electric line which was to transmit electricity from South Dakota to Wisconsin. It was an in-depth conversation which left me realizing how I take electricity for granted.

When I arrived in Minneapolis, I boarded the light rail for downtown where my son-in-law was to meet me. On one of the stops a black man came on the train. He met a woman who was his girlfriend or related in some way. I thought at first he had some mental problem as he was talking and talking and I could not understand him. He took out his phone and continued talking. I then realized that he was rapping and the rhythm of the words pulsated through the speech. His female companion was at the same time going through his wooly hair with a small comb. They left the train before I did. All I could think was how limited and sheltered a life I live.

This is the story of burying my sister's ashes. May she rest in peace.

ME

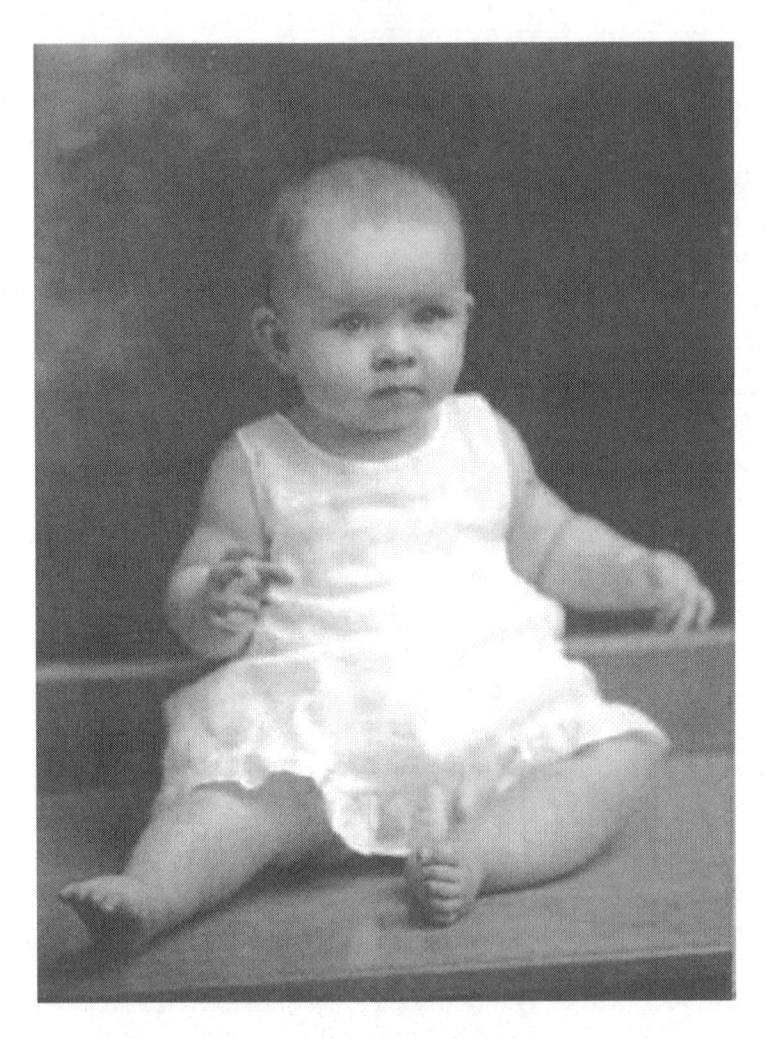

I was born November 4, 1933, right in the middle of the Great Depression. I always said I was born because of FDR, Franklin Delano Roosevelt. I say this because when FDR was elected he expanded the agricultural programs to help the farmers who were really hurting from the severe economic problems of the Depression. He created the AAA, the Agricultural Adjustment Administration. The purpose of the agency was to control the production of crops because of the surplus that had been created due to the diminished amount of trade during the Depression. Agricultural extension agents oversaw the AAA employees and worked with the University of Minnesota in carrying out the programs. County Agricultural Agents were employees of the University and the county where they were hired.

Thus it was my parents moved to Willmar where my father had a job. They lived first in a cabin on Eagle Lake. They then moved into an upstairs apartment on Second Street East. A family named Coursin owned the house and rented out the upstairs.

Later we moved to Ann Street and lived in a first floor apartment. Nana and Grandpa Ostrom lived above us in the upstairs apartment.

The first memory I have is looking out a bedroom window with wonderful starched organdy curtains. There was an empty lot next door which gradually ascended into a hill. The neighborhood elementary students would cut through a lot which had a very worn path to go to Lincoln Elementary School. My memories do not go back into my babyhood very far. I was probably three and a half by the time I remember anything. I was eager to join the students climbing the path.

Willmar did have half day kindergarten and so when I was five I began attending school. I can't remember the teacher's name. What I do remember is that I lost my breakfast every day before I went to school. My mother would fill me with oatmeal and each day I would vomit it up. I also cried a lot at school. Once I couldn't get my snow boots on. They were tight and I have never been very handy. Also my mother probably spoiled me and so I didn't learn to put them on for myself. Another time I cried because I wore a coat to school and no one else did.

School was an ordeal for me. My crying continued on through first, second, and third grade. I couldn't keep my breakfast down either. My first grade teacher was Miss Heine. She was an old maid and didn't much like children. She was also my second grade teacher. My third grade teacher was Miss Mitfitt and I don't think she liked children much either.

One of my worst crying spells came in third grade. We were shown a film to encourage tooth brushing. In this film was shown the effects of tooth decay. It was depicted in a snakelike image winding its way through the tooth and destroying it. Now be certain my mother saw to it that I brushed my teeth twice a day. I don't remember when I had my first cavity, but I don't think I had more than one or two small cavities by this time. Most of my cavities were in my molars. At any rate the thought of this serpentine monster twisting its way through my teeth was more than I could stand. I cried and I cried and I cried. Miss Mittfit finally called my mother who walked to school and brought me home.

The next year we were fortunate to have a caring teacher, Miss Nelson. She was blond and wore her hair in an upsweep. She had a very crooked nose, but all in all she was quite attractive. She even married at the end of the school year. This, of course, meant she couldn't teach any longer. Married women were not allowed to teach.

My mother belonged to a bridge club. I never particularly liked the women in that group. We had a black board

Bev and Barb

hanging in our kitchen. We used it for messages or practicing math or grocery lists or whatever. I came down to the kitchen on the day after my mother entertained her bridge club. There was caricature of me on the blackboard drawn by one of the members. It was labeled with my name and it said "homely." Why any grown woman would do this to a child I don't know. It hurt terribly. I didn't have a very good image of myself anyway. I thought of this often. Maybe that is why I never learned to play bridge and always shunned such groups of women.

Grade five was not a bad year as far as school was concerned. Miss Oversea, our teacher, encouraged us to read and read and read. Since this was my strong point, I read the most books of anyone in her fifth grade classroom. This was one of my few achievements in school although I think I was probably one of the top people in the class. I've never been able to stand making a mistake. My mother taught me well that I must be perfect. Because I never was able to fulfill her expectations, I was always miserable. This also was my fat period. I was about to have a growth spurt and I had put on a lot of weight. I was teased. "Fatty, fatty, two by four can't get through the kitchen door." With all that reading I was probably not getting enough exercise either.

Sixth grade at Lincoln School, I had a teacher named Miss Person. She was in every degree a professional. I think I learned a lot from her. However she also was the elementary principal and was out of the room a lot. That meant we talked and acted out a lot, even inhibited me. I just made certain I was never caught. Now that I have taught myself, I think how overburdened with duties she was. She coped very well with too many duties and too much responsibility. She didn't have much time to be warm and caring. I didn't much like her, but she was nevertheless a very good teacher.

At this time I was growing rapidly. I reached my adult height of five feet seven inches. I now am very happy with this height, but being the tallest in my class was not great. My peers would not stretch up for a year or two. I had also started to have my menstrual periods. My mother had informed me about this ahead of time, but nevertheless it was a shock and a burden. It was worse for my very intelligent friend, Shirley, however. She was overly endowed and teased cruelly by the males in the classroom. I have never suffered that misfortune.

Seventh grade meant a change of building. We joined the junior/senior high school. We went from class to class and had many teachers. We also had more classmates as the students from Garfield and Lafayette joined with us. Lincoln school students were sort of in the middle of the socio-economic ladder. The richest students came from Garfield School and the poorest from Lafayette School. There wasn't really all that much difference in those days. But the richest always stood out. Money speaks. We were all white and mostly Scandinavian and German. With my Irish descent I was strictly out of place. My friends were far more taciturn and even tempered. I have always had manic periods of outburst, of anger, sorrow, and joy and this was completely out of place.

I had a terrible crush on a male student in my math class. I knew he was very smart, but he skipped school a lot. He didn't get very good grades because of this. Being the era it was, I started making deliberate mistakes because I didn't want to appear to be smarter than he was. Females were never to be better than males at anything particularly math and science and male areas of usual superiority.

I used to walk past Dean's house as often as possible in hopes I would see him. He came from a large family. His father worked at a dry cleaning establishment as a tailor. I don't think they had much money. Dean worked at the bowling alley setting pins from an early age. I used to go there too, although I never bowled. I was always accompanied by friends of course. Once in a great while we would spy a glimpse of him, but not often. Once I tried to call him, but when someone in his house answered, I immediately hung up.

As I say Dean was very smart although he was not a very good student. One day I came to school and heard he was performing an experiment which involved gun powder. It had blown up in his face. I went home and vomited. I was sick for two days. Finally I had to return to school. He returned also with what looked like an extreme sunburn and as young people often do returned to his former appearance quickly.

I had crush on Dean for years. Even after I was married I would think of him. I recently had a dream in which I saw his mother. I thought I remembered that woman in the dream. I don't know if I am right or not. She wore very old fashioned dresses and she was not very good looking, but she carried herself proudly and took no second position among the parents of the students. She wore very orthopedic shoes which had a slight heel. She was quite tall. Whether my dream showed her as she was or not, she could easily have been Dean's mother with her obvious intelligence and high self esteem.

Oh, I forgot to say, Dean began smoking at a very early age. In seventh grade he was known as "Dean, Dean, the nicotine queen." My favorite song was Jerome Kern's "Smoke Gets in Your Eyes."

My ninth grade year was rather uneventful. I remember our

Algebra teacher, Mr. Iverson. He spoke loudly and had great discipline. The male students really liked him. His son was a classmate of my sister, Barb. I was still thinking it was not a good idea for a girl to get good grades in math. It ruined all chances with the opposite sex and I was really interested in boys. I did quite badly on a test on purpose. I did not want to look too good. Mr. Iverson called me in to talk to me. He said he knew that I could do all these problems and he was puzzled why I did so badly. He changed my grade on this opinion of his. I received an A in the class anyway. This seems quite unbelievable now, but I think I remember it correctly.

It was about this time that my father had a serious heart attack. It occurred while he was at work at the office. He did not feel well and closed the office door, because he did not want anyone to see him ill. By some miracle someone knocked on the door and went into the room and became aware that he was very ill. The hospital was very near and he was taken there and received immediate care. He survived by the grace of God. The McCamus males did not have strong hearts nor did my grandmother, Eliza Boyles McCamus. He was fortunate and so were the other members of the family.

My father changed his lifestyle. He designated more night meetings to his staff. He walked to work and home again. He took a nap at noon. He also, on the doctor's recommendation, had a drink of whiskey each evening before supper, which is what we called it then. My mother who was a teetotaler accepted this, I guess because it was doctor's orders.

My strongest memory of this was one day when I came home for lunch, my father, was not feeling well. Lunch hours were very long in those days. I think we had almost an hour and a half. I called the doctor. Doctors were still making house calls in those days. I stayed with my father until Dr. Hodapp arrived at the house. He looked my father over and then told me to go back to school. I was already late, but I returned to see the assistant principal for an excuse. Most of the students were quite afraid of Mr. Rowheder. He was quite handicapped with a very twisted back and a terrible limp. He made up for his physical disabilities with a very gruff and tough manner. He knew my father as they were both Kiwanis members and had talked often. He must have known that my father had had a heart attack. I was almost never late, maybe once or twice. I wasn't perfect. Nevertheless he gave me a stern lecture complete with threats that this path would lead to expulsion. Since I thought I had done the right thing, I don't think his words made me very contrite. I don't really like being disciplined and I usually felt very remorseful and cried. I didn't this time.

I had another incident with Mr. Rohweder. He taught ninth grade civics. I think he was a so-so teacher. I don't remember him being particularly bad or good. When grades were handed out at one six weeks period, I received a C in Civics. I didn't think I probably would get an A, but I didn't think I deserved a C either. I bolstered my courage and went in to ask him if this was the correct grade. He looked through his record book and indeed decided that that was not the grade recorded there. I think the C belonged to the girl who sat behind me. He had somehow mixed them up. He did change the grade to a B, but maybe it should even have been an A.

Mr. Rohweder had a beautiful red haired wife who seemed to take very good care of him. They remained married for the rest of his life as far as I know. I think he died fairly young, however, perhaps in his fifties. I don't really remember that.

I really liked my tenth grade English teacher, Miss Struthers. She was an excellent literature teacher. I still remember a lot of what she taught about Dickens' *A Tale of Two Cities* when I went on to read *Great Expectations* on my own. She also taught us Shakespeare's *Julius Caesar* so well I have reread it a number of times. Miss Struthers had lovely premature gray hair and a bad complexion. She, however, had a sensational figure which the boys in the class commented on often, not to her face, of course. She lived with the physical education teacher. I think Miss Rosentreter was a very good phy ed teacher. Since I was so bad at anything physical, I wouldn't know. Everything but volley ball was torture for me. Because I was so tall, I was a fairly good volley ball player. Now Miss Rosentretter was not very feminine. She was straight and muscley, short haired with strong carved features. I never thought much about this, but I had a friend from church who was considered not very feminine either and she brought up the fact that Miss Struthers and Miss Rosentretter were a homosexual couple. This didn't seem to be much of a problem to parents or the community. During the war, that is World War II when we were fighting the Germans, there was great suspicion surrounding Miss Rosentretter. Some people doubted her patriotism because of her German name and her German heritage. Although there was much talk about this, nothing ever came of it. Miss Rosentretter served on state committees for her contributions and expertise on physical education. Both Miss Struthers and Miss Rosentretter were excellent teachers and fortunately remained at the school until they retired.

I think I haven't mentioned Miss Emery. Miss Emery was the math teacher for Geometry and Trigometry. My student friends all called her the best teacher in the high school. My friend, Shirley, who was an equal of Miss Emery in math abilities, thought very highly of her. I have always been a better English and Social Studies student than math student. I didn't have to pretend to be a worse Geometry student than the males in my class. I actually was. We had to memorize theorems word for word and Miss Emery would call us to the board to write them out. I could memorize and so I always received an A, but I didn't understand Geometry at all and I often sat with tears of frustration through the whole class. Miss Emery was in charge of the Honor Society. The next year I was inducted into it. This was mostly due to my friends, Shirley and Gloria, who were super students and helped me all the time. Miss Emery had me read the character part of the qualities of Honor Students. I have always thought this was strange, because if anyone ever knew me, they would know I was a terrible fraud.

In Eleventh Grade, I had Mr. Wahlstrand for an American History teacher. Mr. Wahlstrand had been our neighbor. He and his family lived on Fourth Street right behind us. He had snow white hair and the story went around that his hair had turned white overnight in the trenches during World War I. Mr. Wahlstrand was a representative in the Minnesota State Legislature which met every other year then I think. He had a leave of absence from teaching for the two to three months the body was in session. He was extremely Conservative. Party labels were not given at the time, but he was far to the right. This was very detectable in his class. He detested Franklin Delano Roosevelt. I remember him pounding on the table with his fist and saying "and Roosevelt thought he was God." Since I was born because of the policies of FDR this did not sit well with me. Then Mr. Wahlstrand did not like Indians either. He thought they were lazy and stupid and a real drag on good Scandinavian Americans. Actually he didn't mention the Scandinavians. They just made up a large proportion of Willmar's citizens and so it was implied. We had some Indian, that's what we called them at the time, students in the class. They were perhaps half breeds, but they had a fair amount of Indian blood. I also had Indian blood, but not a lot. My great grandmother was a quarter Indian, so it was quite diluted when it came to me. Most of the students weren't very political and so weren't bothered much by Mr. Wahlstrand. Some of them just took a nap, because he was pretty boring. He would ask about five to seven questions during the hour class. He went in alphabetical order around the class, row by row. It was easy to figure when the question would be asked of you. So the day, your name was to come up you studied hard and the rest of the time you could day-dream. I had just one anxiety which kept my anger in check. My father was an employee of the University of Minnesota, Kandiyohi County, and the State of Minnesota. Mr. Wahlstrand had some influence over his job and his salary and I understood I needed to get along for my own well being. Thus I behaved myself, pretty much.

It was junior-senior prom year. I wasn't dating and so expected to go with my female friends to the dance. In Willmar, the prom was only for junior and senior students of the school. In other words, your date had to be a member of one of the two classes. The junior class president that year was Don Stock. He was having a hot affair with a very sexy freshman girl. He had to have a date, because he had to lead the grand march. I was available and acceptable, so he asked me to go with him. I didn't really know him well and I didn't want the stigma of not having a date, so I accepted. It was a wretched night. He paid no attention to me. We led the

Grand March and we stayed a bit. Then he took me home and dumped me to go to an after prom party with his hot freshman girlfriend. I joined my female friends who I should have gone with in the first place.

When I was a senior, the prom scenario was reversed. This time I had a boyfriend who was not a junior or senior at Willmar High. I had a good friend named Dora Jean Grams. Sometimes we called her Dodie. She had somewhere met Bob Magaard whose father owned a farm just outside Willmar, a dairy farm. Bob as the oldest of seven males had taken over the farming operation. His brother Omar was in our class, Dora Jean's and mine. Bob was six or eight years older, I don't remember which just now. Anyway Bob was a Golden Gloves boxer. He had a friend, Art Werder who was also a Golden Gloves boxer. Both of them also attended the Missouri Synod Lutheran church. We usually made a foursome and attended a lot of baseball games and activities in town. Art was a very kind and gentle fellow. He worked with his two of his older brothers in construction. They built houses in the area, fairly modest houses and homes for their fellow church members.

During the summer the four of us went to Lake Okoboji to the amusement park. Bob's brother just younger than he was, Junior, lived there and was married. We visited him and had good time riding the rides. We also went to the Aquatennial celebration in Minneapolis to watch the parade. We had some good times together. This was 1950 and the Korean War had begun. Bob was exempt from the draft. I don't remember if it was because he was farming or if he had a minor medical problem. Art, however, was drafted. I had started attending classes at the U that fall. He asked me to marry him and knowing no better I accepted. He gave me an engagement ring. He was sent to Korea, but I'm not certain how much combat he saw. I decided I just couldn't marry him. He had not graduated from high school and I was in an exciting new world of academics. I knew a marriage with him could not work. I have felt guilty ever since, but I returned his ring when he was in Korea.

Fortunately he came home and married a young woman I had worked with at the S&L Department Store the summer after I completed my junior year in high school. She was very pleasant and a good companion. I probably introduced them. I don't remember. Anyway they married soon after he returned home. They had two children before he was diagnosed with leukemia and died. He was only in his thirties and it was tragic. I have always had great remorse over the whole situation, but it would have been a great mistake to have married him.

I had entered the University as a Home Economics major. I lived in an ancient dorm on the St. Paul Campus my freshman year. I had two roommates and since I was the last to arrive I was assigned the top bunk. My mother was extremely concerned about this. She was afraid I would fall out. I had had some sleepwalking incidents at home, not many, just a couple, but my mother was always overprotective. I managed just fine. One of my roommates was not interested in college at all, but completed her freshman year and went home and was married. My other roommate, Sally Gustafson, was from Kandiyohi County. She was two years older as she had worked before she entered college. She was a good Methodist and at the end of the year both of us moved to the newly built Methodist Student House on Cleveland Avenue. We were never very close. We weren't interested in the same areas. She graduated in Home Ec and became a Home Agent I think. I sort of lost track of her.

I found the beginning courses in Home Ec quite easy. I also took introductory courses in Psychology and Chemistry. All of this was fine, but I liked the electives I took in American History and Humanities much better. I used up all my electives by the time I finished the first quarter of my sophomore year. This was also the crisis time in my engagement period with Art Werder.

I had spent the summer working at the Willmar State Hospital. I was placed in the medical ward at the hospital which meant the patients I dealt with were both mentally and physically ill. The only training I received was with the R.N. who was in charge of the unit. She was all right, but rather brusque and impersonal. I don't think she cared if I knew anything or not. The truth was that this was a completely alien world to me. Luther Youngdahl was governor of the State of MInnesota and with his leadership the mental health system and the state hospitals were beginning to be reformed. Nevertheless they hired green college students like me to step in when the regular employees were on vacation.

I remember vividly my first experience. I was to assist in cleaning up a four hundred pound woman who was bedridden and had had a large bowel movement that had been liberally distribute through the bed clothes. We had to turn her, replace the sheets on the bed and bathe her. I think there were three of us, but it was quite a task because she would not or could not help us. Someone managed to help finish the work and then I excused myself and went to the employee bathroom and vomited.

I also had to give injections something I had never done and did not do after my stint at the hospital. I remember having to give injections to a woman who kept saying, "There is too much yeast in the bread. There is too much yeast in the bread!" This was very loud and I thought an indication that I was hurting her, giving her much pain.

I was often given the task of taking patients to entertainment offered at the hospital for those who were mobile enough to go. I enjoyed the movies and the music with the patients and this was usually a good assignment. They also sometimes had dances. I would dance with the patients if they wanted me to dance with them. The best polka partner I have ever had was a large boned woman who weighed at least two hundred pounds who whirled me around the floor at the speed of a rocket. She had great control and it was the best polka dance I have ever had. I took patients to church as well. One time I picked up clients from the chemical dependency unit. Most of them were alcoholics trying to become sober of their own volition or because they had been sentenced by the courts. Often times they were so remorseful and emotional I had to take them back to their rooms.

The reason I had found the job at the hospital was that I had a friend from our Methodist Youth Fellowship group who was also attending the U. She had found out about the summer jobs and they paid very well for young students like Jean and me. Now Jean was very obviously a lesbian. She, I'm sure, received a lot of grief for this. She dressed in a very macho style, so she appeared to advertise her sexual orientation. I enjoyed her company because she was very intelligent and also very different. I have never been entirely conventional. I loved males and did not have lesbian tendencies, I think. Anyway Jean worked in the chemical dependency unit. There was a small number of what we then called drug addicts from the Twin Cities. Jean became enamored of one them and the two ran off together before the summer was over. This relationship did not last long. I saw Jean only once after that. She moved to New Orleans and was studying fungi she said. She was quite unusual.

I returned to the University with multiple contradictions in my life. First of all, I did not want to marry Art Werder. I just couldn't. I sent the ring back and ended the engagement. Then I did not want to major in Home Ec. I felt I was badly misplaced. I had neither the skills nor the interest in Home Economics. I liked to cook and I have always been involved with food and eating. However, I didn't find my ability as a cook should be founded on how well I peeled an orange. It seemed trivial to me. I also couldn't connect food and costs. It was not that I had extravagant tastes. I just didn't want to figure the cost of a tablespoon of flour or a pinch of salt. I really didn't like my Foods instructor and I think I got a C in the class.

My father was insistent that I have an employable education. Besides Barb was four years younger than I was and was a much more intelligent and dedicated student. I had to graduate in four years. I was obviously in a pickle. There were three occupations open to females, teaching, nursing, and clerical work. After my stint at the State Hospital, I knew I did not want to be a nurse. I had done some clerical work at my father's office during school vacations and this did not lure me either. I thought it was boring. That left teaching as the only choice for an occupation. I didn't want to do that either, but it seemed the best of the alternatives.

I studied the University's class offerings and the courses needed to achieve a degree. I found a lot of Humanities and History courses I would like to take. When I was looking in the requirements for a teaching degree, I found a listing called Core Curriculum. It was a somewhat radical approach to education. It was led by a man named Nelson Boswell who taught in the Education Department at the U. Some of his ideas are still being kicked around by scholars and school reformers. Core Curriculum combined the classes in English, Social Studies, and Science into one three hour block with the subjects intertwining rather than being taught as separate entities. It had attractions to me. I always like new ideas and experimenting. It seemed like an intriguing plan. It also would allow me to graduate on time, because I had some Science credits in Chemistry, Physics, and Biology. I had a lot of history credits and even some in Social Science. My Humanities credits were acceptable for the English classes. I had always taken eighteen to twenty credits or almost always, so I had a lot of credits. I probably would have had better grades if I had taken fewer credits, but I usually managed to eke out B's. I could finish time with attending one summer session. This was my way to accommodate my father's wishes and I would not completely be separated from my true interests.

Several issues were also developing in my social life. Joan Ryan had moved into the Methodist Student House. Joan was always a stickler for following the rules. This was the fifties and women still had hour limits on how late they could stay out at night. Week days, females had to be in at 10:00 p.m. and on weekends. Friday and Saturday, the hour was moved to 12:00 p.m. My parents did not have strict hours for me at home, so this was a disruption to me. I like to discuss and argue. Often I was deep into some conundrum at ten o'clock or even twelve o'clock. Odd person that I am, I have never liked social rules. I understand laws and safety rules and rules enacted for the consideration of others, but social rules have always seemed stupid to me. I have a rebellious streak as well. Strangely I think this comes from my mother. She followed no rules when she was young, but then when she married my father, I think she tried too hard to fit in with the McCamus snobbishness. Who knows of what they had to be so proud, but they were proud.

Anyway Joan was always complaining that I came in too late. I was violating hours. Since I like peace and I like to get along with people mostly. I tried to come in on time. When I was a senior Joan was house manager. She always liked to run things, and being a good Conservative loved to be the enforcer of the rules. I was less and less controlled by the rules, so we had a confrontation now and then. Not much was done about my infractions, however, because the couple who were our house chaperones were busy working and studying. They also probably didn't find it the most compelling issue before them.

I was dating some then too. I was going with a veterinary

medicine student named Harry Balas. He lived near Benson and he would often give me rides home as he went through Willmar. He was a good dancer and we went to some dances together. He was also working at a veterinary clinic on Raymond Avenue and I would go there with him. Veterinary Medicine is a difficult career. He was struggling with his classes and his advisor suggested he needed to study harder and it might be a good idea if he dropped his girlfriend, me. At least this is what he told me. I never found evidence it wasn't true. This didn't really break my heart. I liked him, but I didn't want a serious relationship either. Years later he called my mother's house in Willmar. Barb and John were there. Don and I had gone out and John answered the phone. Harry's father was in the Willmar Hospital and he had called to ask how life was going for me. He was a kind and generous fellow and again a Missouri Synod Lutheran. Why I kept going with males of that religious persuasion I do not know. I found his obituary recently. He lived near Minot or was it Bismark, North Dakota, and the obituary mentioned his accomplishments both as veterinarian and as a member of the community.

I haven't mentioned that the Methodist Student House had a large dining room in the lower level. We had an organized meal program. We paid for the food and did the cooking and clean up ourselves. As many as fifty people could be fed at a time. Only twelve females lived in the house, but a large number of males were involved in the meal program. One of the senior home ec students made up the menus and ordered the food. We signed up for cooking and clean up duties and everyone who ate participated. It worked pretty well as well as human endeavors work. My roommate, Cleone Luchau, liked to cook, but would have nothing to do with clean up. I did a bit of both.

I dated a couple of the fellows who ate at the coop. One was Phil, a forester, whose last name I can't remember. He was not very good looking, but he was pleasant and kind. I also dated Darrel Scheerhorn who had a visible wine port birthmark on his forehead. He was younger than I was and he seemed a bit immature. He later married one of the girls who ate at the coop. I ran into him at Farmfest a long time later. He had had the birthmark removed, but still had a bit of a scar. He was working for Pioneer Seeds I believe. He was an Agronomy major I think.

Somehow I managed to graduate from the University with a Core Curriculum major in June, 1955. I had to persuade a professor in the English Department that my credits in Rhetoric in the College of Agriculture, Forestry, Home Economics and Veterinary Medicine would satisfy the requirements for freshman English. I still don't know how I convinced this very adamant man that I could graduate.

Practice teaching was torture for me. I sometimes walked through the fairgrounds to an elementary school in the Como Avenue area. It was a grade one through eight school and I taught eighth graders. It is all very blurry to me. The teacher I taught under was very motherly and shepherded me through the experience. Then I taught ninth graders also in a St. Paul School. Another Core Curriculum major was also practice teaching there. He was a large very confident young man who had all the answers. He drove me crazy with his bragging of his abilities and intelligence. The teacher I taught under accused me of putting him down. I probably did, but he was truly obnoxious. The teacher was excellent, but I was so nervous it was extremely difficult for me. My third practice teaching assignment was at Marshall High School near the U campus. There were a lot of professors' kids in the class. They all knew more than I did. I think one of them was the son of the Jewish man who talks about Minnesota history of TPT and MPR. I also think I may have taught one of the women who now lives down the hall in the Realife Cooperative. Fortunately, although the years coincide, she does not remember me.

I was immensely surprised to receive a letter from the Superintendent of Schools in Winnebago. He was interested in establishing a Core program in Winnebago. He wondered if I would be interested and would come for an interview. It so surprised me that anyone at all would consider me as a teacher that I immediately wrote back and arranged for the meeting. Since I wanted to move out of the Twin Cities at the time, I accepted the job offer. I would be teaching two hour core classes, one sophomore English class, and a language arts class. I was also to direct two class plays, a one act play for the speech contest. I would be eighth grade class advisor, sell tickets for football and basketball games, and perform any other tasks that might arise.

I found a room in which to live. It was a large finished attic room which I was to share with the librarian, Lou Wiens. Mrs. Porter was the landlady's name. She was Judy Hanks' grandmother. We had breakfast privileges there. This was cold breakfast of cereal, toast, and juice. Mrs. Porter was grumpy and pretty religious. She did, however, go to the Methodist Church which was a plus in my favor. The other plus was that she did not like Lou Wiens. Lou was a Mennonite from Mountain Lake. She also was engaged to be married to Roger Stauffer. Roger had served in the Korean War. He was a hero. He had saved a man from drowning in the Yalu River. Mrs. Porter didn't know why any self respecting woman would marry into that Stauffer family. I believe Roger's father was an alcoholic.

I had problems with Lou completely unrelated to Mrs. Porter's problems with her. First of all we had to sleep in the same bed. The mattress was not of the best quality and had a deep dip in the middle. This kept us separated at least. The problem was sometimes in the night I would roll over and move into the dip. This was too close to Lou, so she would push me out of the hole. I would have preferred she had awakened me and asked me to move. She was aggressive and she pushed hard. Then she went home every weekend. Now that seems strange to me, since Roger was in Winnebago. She left her clothes and the sewing projects she worked on all over the room. I was pretty much stuck there in her mess. The worst problem was that she was extremely Conservative. She taught two English classes. She taught one semester of grammar and the other semester she taught very old literature. She did not believe in Core Curriculum and let me know that she did not. Neither of us fit the community particularly well I think.

I was also still dating. I somehow ran in to a fellow from Willmar, the adopted son of a dentist there. His name was Jerry Mertz. I wasn't particularly interested in him, but we had Willmar memories and news to discuss.

My cousin by marriage, Manny Brothren also came to visit. He was a wonderful musician and played the piano in dance halls and bars from the time he was a teenager. He was three years younger than I was. His father, who was an alcoholic, had died in a mobile home fire in Alaska. Manny's mother, Aileen, married my Uncle George who was by this time in his fifties. She was a full blooded Finn and this was often brought up by the family. They didn't really approve of her and it seemed a bad match. Actually it was. They were right. Manny and Aileen were a fortress against my Uncle George, who was a pretty easy going guy. Manny, who took after his biological father, drank a lot. Eventually he assaulted George and a divorce followed. It was bad for Aileen because she had no money. She ended up scrubbing floors in the rooming house where she lived and died young of cancer. Manny graduated from Witchita State University in Kansas and taught music for many years in Bagley apparently with the help of his wife who kept him in line. I never met her because by the time they married we were more or less estranged as a family.

The faculty in Winnebago was very congenial, particularly the high school faculty. We had parties after football and basketball games at the homes of mostly the married teachers. Their wives were wonderful cooks and didn't work at a paying job, so they prepared the food. We had a drink or two and ate roasted chicken and fried pheasant and beef sandwiches. We talked and joked and the parties were enjoyable.

One night Don and Maurice Sonnicksen showed up at a school dance in the auditorium. The Ag teacher, Marv Theisse, who is a cousin of Judy Terhune's actually was the chaperone. He suggested that Don and Maurice go to the Bob Thompson house and join the faculty party there. Bob was an English teacher who was very intelligent and very lazy. They did go to the party much to the consternation of one of the teacher's wives who called them party crashers.

I had actually met Don before at the Bass Lake Ballroom when I went to that forbidden spot with Gene Shepherd. All of those young men had just returned from being drafted into the Korean Conflict and they were home and restless. Winnebago in those days was a good place to meet young men.

There is a running disagreement between Don and me about

who was the instigator of the relationship, but he took me home, all of about six blocks and we began dating. That is the story of how we found each other.

DON

I didn't decide to go to Winnebago to teach because of the high proportion of males to females there. I moved to Winnebago because I was asked by Jerome Webster, the superintendent of schools, to try a new concept in teaching which was called Core Curriculum. This was my major at the University of Minnesota. The controversial idea was to combine the teaching of English, Social Studies, and Science. In Winnebago it was asked that the program be used in eighth grade English and Geography. I was so happy to have the opportunity for a job in my field outside of the Twin Cities area that I signed the contract. I also was to direct two class plays and a one-act contest play. This was in addition to being eighth grade class advisor, supervising homecoming float construction, and selling tickets for sports and music events.

I was young and I have always overestimated the amount of work I could do. This was going to be challenging.

I had been told by my Aunt Ina who had married my Uncle Carl and was herself a Home Economics teacher, that young female teachers were very popular in small communities. This turned out to be true especially at this period of time. It was 1955 and the Korean War had ended or at least an armistice had been signed. A number of U. S. draftees who had completed their two years of service were discharged at this time. Winnebago's share of draftees returned home. There seemed to be a lot of young bachelors around. Some of them were farmers. Some of them were still college students and some of them held jobs in the area.

I don't remember how I met Gene. I was probably introduced. He was finishing a business degree at St. Thomas, but spent time at home with his parents. We started dating. This seemed to meet the approval of a lot local residents, my landlady, the teachers and the general public. Gene's father had a good position with Interstate Power then with headquarters in Winnebago. His mother was a nurse at the local hospital. He had an outgoing personality and was well liked. One time he asked if I would like to go to a dance at the Bass Lake Ballroom. This was about five miles out of town. It had, at one time, been a Baptist Camp. I don't know if it was Dudley Riggs and his mother who opened it as an entertainment venue or if they were just among the first people who owned it. The story was that they had circus acts there. I'm not sure.

Anyway, it was now a ballroom and had a reputation for being a bit wild. There was the story of the woman who had a fight with her boyfriend and knocked him out cold. He was probably intoxicated at the time and she was somewhat burly. There was bootleg liquor sold there as they did not have a liquor license. Then Gene said a lot of spouses did not return home with the person to whom they were married.

Teachers were not supposed to go there. They weren't supposed to go to the American Legion either. At least the women teachers were not to be seen in either establishment.

Now I am not one who takes restrictions easily. I could determine no good reason why I should not attend a dance at the Bass Lake Ballroom. On a Saturday night it was the gathering place for all the lively young people, if they weren't Baptist and forbidden to dance. I thought about it a bit and said I would go.

I was slightly apprehensive about it as I don't really like to get into trouble, but I went anyway. My first observation was that there were many parents of my students there dancing and consuming alcohol and seemingly having a good time. Did teachers have more of an influence on the young than the parents?

We joined the group of Gene's friends. I danced with him. He was not a very good dancer and didn't seem to care if he danced or not. Then I danced with some of his friends. One of the best of the dancers was a fellow named Don. We danced well together. Later when we were sitting in a booth he pulled me down on his lap and gave me his ribbon tie which was advertising the Winnebago Centennial which was to be celebrated that summer.

I'm not certain when Gene and I stopped dating. He had taken me to my parents' home in Willmar once. My mother did not like drinking at all. My father had had a heart attack about five years before this occasion. The doctor had prescribed a drink before dinner to my father because he was a rather tense, though congenial person. He had a demanding job and he was very conscientious. The day Gene and I arrived my mother had baked an angel food cake. She had placed the tube pan upside down on my father's bottle of whiskey so the cake could cool and be removed from the pan. Gene was very excited about this as he really liked to drink. Unfortunately the only person who drank in my family was my father because of doctor's orders.

Gene was very politically Conservative. He was also Catholic. I was neither. Besides that, my family didn't drink. Three strikes against me. Besides that, we had no money.

Gene began dating another teacher who was Catholic was Conservative and her father owned a farm and had money. He called me a bonehead and we parted. I was terribly hurt and really liked him, but I didn't like him enough to change my religion or my politics or anything else about me. It turned out to be the best thing that ever happened to me.

One night some of the teachers went to a movie at the local theater. Right in front of us sat a group of young men, one of whom was Don. I admit it. I tapped him on the shoulder and started flirting. He seemed a little surprised like he didn't remember me and he didn't really respond much.

Winnebago was a small town. The population was under 2500 people. There wasn't a whole lot to do other than the movies or the local dances. Young people often went to Mankato or perhaps even Fairmont for entertainment. However, they couldn't do that all the time. That is why one Friday night Don and a friend were looking for something to do and spotted lights at the High School. They stopped in and chatted with the agriculture teacher who was chaperoning the dance.

On Friday nights the teachers usually gathered after school events at the home of one of the married teachers for a party. Single women teachers were invited as were the few single male teachers. The ag teacher suggested that Don and his friend, Maurice, join the party which was that particular night at the home of the English teacher and his wife. That is what they did.

Dietz

One of teacher's wives was livid. "I hate party crashers", she protested. "What are they doing here? Nobody invited them."

They had, of course, been invited by the ag teacher who came after the school dance was concluded, but that didn't really count. We drank a little, ate some, and talked a lot. It was as usual a mostly pleasant affair.

There is some dispute about what happened at the end of the evening. Don said I waited around for him to give me a ride home. My memory was that he asked to take me home. This many years later it doesn't matter I guess. I don't know what happened to Maurice, but Don took me home. That was the beginning.

We dated a lot. We went to movies, out for dinner, to dances all around Winnebago and in Mankato and Fairmont and street dances in the summer. I had never had so much fun. My mother was very strict. My boyfriends were pretty dull.

Don was farming with his father at the time and living at home. His youngest brother was a student of mine and thought Don was crazy for dating me. The farm they farmed was on Highway 169 and visible from the road. Somewhere along the line I mentioned how straight the corn rows were in his field. This was a magic comment. Farmers were always discussing how straight the corn rows were in everyone's fields. Why I said this I do not know. What did I know about rows of field corn anyway?

The days and months passed. I left for the summer, but Don came to see me in Willmar. He was working hard in those days, but he was still great company. We had lots of stimulating conversation and his sense of humor was original. We didn't agree on everything. I was more liberal than he was and once we had an argument about Negros which is what blacks or African Americans were called at that time. I told him to stop the car, because I was going to get out and walk. He just kept talking to me and convinced me that we were not as far apart in our thinking as I believed. He was very good at this although in the end, a long time later, he agreed with me.

Our favorite Don story is this. Our second daughter, Eilene, became a chemical engineer. She had taken a position with Cargill at Raleigh, North Carolina. When Don went to the local Cargill Elevator, the manager and the laborers there were teasing him. They said that if she went to Raleigh she would probably end up marrying a black man. This was serious to most people who lived in Winnebago. Don immediately replied, "That's all right as long as he's not a Republican". The men shook their heads and walked away. How Don got by with remarks like that I do not know. Those elevator guys really liked him even after that.

Back to our story, Don's and mine, he asked me to marry him sometime after we met. I wasn't sure I wanted to get married. I wasn't sure I would make a very good farmer's wife for one thing. I didn't really want to stay in Winnebago for another. My good friend, the home economics teacher, was going to Europe for several weeks. I wanted to go to Europe. Don's mother didn't really like me much. My friend and college roommate did not like Don. The whole idea of getting married under these conditions did not seem like a good idea.

Don was very persuasive. He really wouldn't let me say no. I was, in a way, relieved to be out of the dating game. Both of us had had relationships that just did not work out for one reason or another. We were tired of that back and forth stuff. Besides we did get along well and we had fun together and laughed a lot. Everyone thought he had married up because I had an education and was a teacher. He did not go on to college as two of his brothers had. They became English teachers also. After a while I realized that he knew much more than I did. He taught me. He showed how impatient I really am. He put up with my depressions and my erratic behavior, my crying spells and my excessive anger. He made fun of my guilty conscience saying, "You must really think you are important thinking you are responsible for everyone else's problems."

Don was a good farmer and he was good at selling crops at a reasonable price. He never waited for the highest numbers but sold almost always at an above average price. He didn't really care about money. It was mostly about doing things well. We didn't have a lot of cash since what money we had was funneled back into the farming operation. Both of us were content with making enough to raise our daughters. We didn't own land and we didn't want to. Thus I am as close to living in something I own in the Cooperative as I have ever been.

Don was lay leader at the church. He was co-chair of the DFL party in Faribault County and helped elect DFLers to both the Minnesota House of Representatives and the Minnesota Senate in a Republican area.

Was he a perfect husband? Or course not. He occasionally would go on a spree with farmer buddies. He would not appear for supper and I would curse him. Once when I said, "I hate that man". One of our daughters said, "No, you don't, mother." And thus it was.

The American Legion was very important to Don.

Everyone thought we were a strange combination. They couldn't imagine that I would marry Don and they couldn't imagine that he would marry me. Have you ever thought you knew how men and women should pair off? It is always a great mystery. We were married for forty-five years until he died in 2003.

I fit badly in Winnebago, especially at the end when the community became more and more Conservative. I would have liked to have left. I could not. Don loved to farm and I loved him, so I stayed until the next chapter of my life began after his death when I moved to Coon Rapids.

Beverly McCamus Toppin

MY THREE DAUGHTERS

*Kathy in back,
Eilene at left,
Nancy right.*

*Left to right,
Kathy, Eilene and Nancy*

KAKA

Katherine Ann was our first and eagerly awaited child. We had been married only two years when she was born, but I thought I would never get pregnant. It was December 12, 1959 when she was born. Doctor Armstrong was certain that she was early, that she should have born in the first days of January, 1960. As it was she weighed well over eight pounds and so some mistake in calculation must have been made.

It was close to Christmas when we brought her home from the Winnebago Hospital. The stores were open on Main Street and her eyes, even at her wee age, seemed to rove about looking at the lights. I didn't even know how to change her diaper when we arrived home. Fortunately her father was much handier than I was and he changed her the first time.

We lived on the Gray place at the time, called that because Duane Franklin's grandparents owned it. The house was old and cold and drafty in the winter. Don's mother, Florence, had helped paint it and we put in new linoleum and it was light and somewhat pleasant. The water pipes froze, however, when the temperature dropped low enough.

We put Kathy in what we called a bunny suit to sleep at night. If the wind was blowing hard the curtains in the upstairs bedrooms would flutter. Nevertheless she was a very healthy baby.

Don was very proud of his first child and I think he was happy that she was a girl. The *Winnebago Enterprise* noted in a column his pride at having become a father.

Kathy was called by many names. One was Bunny because of the bunny suit I guess. Then after her sisters were born a little bit more than two years and some after four years after she was born, she was called Kaka. I called her Kath mostly.

She learned to talk at a remarkably early age. She jabbered understandably by a year and a half. Being the oldest when her sisters arrived she had to look after them. She was always, or almost always, very responsible.

She seemed to like school and learned easily. She loved music and played the piano and learned the guitar and the saxophone. She managed to get out of class when she was in sixth grade to take guitar lessons from the music teacher. Her classroom teacher was not happy about this and told me so. I replied that she seemed tethered to the guitar. I was not popular and probably she wasn't either.

Because she was the oldest and because all of our daughters had to help on the farm, she did a lot of work. I particularly remember baling hay. Kath was often the one who had the task of putting the bales in the elevator which moved them to the hay mow. They were heavy and she developed muscles doing the work.

Kathy was a good student and good musician. She played the saxophone in the All-State Orchestra and often played solos. She also was page in the Minnesota State Legislature when Henry Kalis was our state representative. She was a wonderful dancer. She and her dancing father would glide across the kitchen floor and it was a pleasure to watch.

Since other members of the family had attended the University of Minnesota, she also enrolled there. She was going to be a music major, but changed her mind and became a German major instead. She spent her junior year studying in Munich, Germany, and became very fluent in the language. She loved the culture and Don and I had a wonderful time visiting her.

Since we had so many English teachers in the family, the Toppin daughters thought it was a family curse. Kath graduated with the German major, but without Education credits. This made it difficult to find a job. She began working at the Nectary in downtown Minneapolis in the City Center. There she met her husband to be, Scott Mugge. Scott was from the Iron Range and had attended Dunwoody to become a draftsman. Scott was training managers for what became a small franchise and they married. They were married at the Wesley Methodist Church, an historic site because it was the first, or one of the first, churches built in Minneapolis.

They moved to Stevens Square where an old area had been renovated and the rent was low. They soon found it was a difficult place to live with cockroaches and large Indian families who lived together in very small quarters. They moved to Brooklyn Center. When Kathy

Don and Elise

became pregnant with Elise they decide this was no place to raise a child and they moved to St. Cloud.

Kathy decided she should obtain teaching credits so she could find a job. She was hired at St. Cloud Cathedral as a German teacher and expanded the program and was working more than full time at her position. Every other year she would take her students to Germany. Don was needed as a male chaperone one year and so again we traveled to Germany. I was to go one more time, the year Don died and Kath asked if I would like to go along on the tour.

Kath always said she married her mother, because Scott and my temperaments were rather the same. We were both moody and tended to look on the dark side of things sometimes. Kath had her father's sunny disposition and his outgoing personality. She was an extremely hard worker and had an affinity for languages. She has always loved learning and she had a gift for teaching.

Being a Liberal and teaching at a Catholic School is not an easy proposition, but she has always been social and liked so she got by with it. She loved the German culture and since St. Cloud had many descendants from Germany, she fit in well. She and two friends made their own beer for a time. They split their product and gave some away. It was good!

It was Kath who told her dad on his death bed that he was "the best Daddy anyone could possibly have ever had." It was surely true. I always think she was a great recipient of his very colorful and pleasing DNA.

MY DAUGHTER EILENE

No one in our family has a soft voice. Sometimes out of self-consciousness, I sound like I have a soft voice. I do not. After I have made the initial plunge I resonate, unfortunately loudly sometimes. My voice can be heard even when the listener does not like to hear it. This also true of all three of my daughters and was also true of my husband.

We went to a lot of dances, Don and I. Often at the end of an especially good dance number Don would yell out loud an echoing "Yahoo!" Although this was slightly embarrassing, it really turned me on. His would also be the most fervent amen in church. He was very political and when he agreed with a political speaker he would shout out, "Yes! Yes! Yes!" Don was not known to be silent spectator. Nevertheless he was far more diplomatic on an individual basis than I have ever managed to be, but he always made his voice heard.

Thus it is not strange that my daughters have voices also, even Nancy our youngest daughter who has borne all the humiliation of the family members who went before her. She sometimes cringes at her mother's and her sisters' outspoken words, but she will shout herself when she feels strongly about something.

Our daughter, Kathy, as her father, is both funny and diplomatic. Her voice is strong and she will shout out and seemingly gets into not much trouble.

Our middle daughter, Eilene, takes after her mother to everyone's dismay including mine. I love my daughter,

Eilene, but somehow she missed the lessons on tact. This is not because she lacks intelligence. She probably scores higher on I.Q. tests than any of us. She is after all, a chemical engineer. No one could call her unassertive. When she was not chosen as a speaker at her high school graduation although she tied for highest honors, she volunteered in such a way that no one could turn her down. She was bound to speak and she did. And she spoke very well, I must say.

It was very difficult for a female to enter a male profession such as engineering in 1985. Eilene was assigned to a soy bean plant at Port Cargill in Savage after being hired by Cargill. I think this incident explains Eilene extraordinarily well. As often happens in bean plants there was spillage. Most of this is taken care of mechanically, but there is a bit of manual labor connected with the cleanup. Some of the employees of the plant were not exactly ambitious, but they were macho males and did not take kindly to a female supervisor. They had come in to drive vehicles and push buttons. Eilene was raised on a farm and taught by her father. When assigning the task of shoveling up a bean spill she had available only two of the more laggard employees. So she grabbed two shovels and she said to them. "I'll take this shovel and you fellows can change off with the other shovel." Shame is a powerful tactic, this I understand.

What I don't understand is the following story. Eilene was moved to Raleigh, North Carolina by Cargill. This has a very nasty political story connected to it, which the family knows, but I won't tell. Yes, I will tell it. I changed my mind. Don had taken a wagon of grain to the Winnebago Elevator. He had lots of red neck friends living there. He had proudly told them that Eilene was going as a chemical engineer to Raleigh. They were mighty teasers. One of them said to

Don, "She will probably marry a black man." He instantly replied, "As long as he's not a Republican." The red necks shook a fist at him and walked away. They still remained friends. Don't ask me why.

At any rate when Eilene was moved to the Cargill plant in North Carolina she was charged with training in new chemical engineers. Most of them were male. Here comes my amazement. She trained in a young engineer by the name of Jeffrey Ording. He is no pushover either. He is an excellent engineer and has ideas of his own. Usually they are softly expressed. But what on earth possessed him to marry my daughter, Eilene? They have been married for a long time and have two children. He does not like confrontations. Explain this!

There are many more but my favorite Eilene story is this from long ago. Eilene was a darling child. She was cute and she was curious and she was fast. She was much too fast for her mother from the time she was able to walk. She spent a lot of time with her dad who was much quicker and more adept and had a lot more energy than her mother. It was thus she survived her childhood.

She was two and a half when her sister, Nancy, was born. I don't know how it occurred that on this particular Sunday, Don stayed home with Nancy while I went to church with Kathy and Eilene, but that is what happened. Eilene was about three. I always dressed up for church and I always dressed the girls in pretty dresses that their grandparents had given them. They wore their shiny patent leather shoes and their hair was beautifully done. On this particular Sunday I had donned my favorite dress. I had also put on a long beaded necklace which went perfectly with it. (No wonder people hated us. God must have thought us irredeemably vain.) Halfway through the church service Eilene had done all the coloring she was going to do and eaten all the Cheerios I had brought along and was walking up and down the pew. I pulled her down on my lap. She immediately became entranced with my long beaded necklace I let her play with it awhile and then the terrible thought came to me that she might pull on it hard enough to break it. We did not have carpeting under the pews and I could just hear the sound of the dropping and rolling of each bead, plunk, plunk, plunk from our back pew slowly, slowly, slowly down through pew after pew to the altar at the front of the church. The minister was in the middle of his vociferous sermon. What would everyone think with this raining of beads down, down, down, down to the altar? I removed the beads as carefully as I could from Eilene's hands. I planned to take them off and put them in my purse. But before I could, Eilene let out a roar of complaint such as I have never heard before in any church by any child. I tried desperately to calm her. She was not to be calmed. After all, she has her mother's temper. She screamed and cried deafeningly. I decided the only solution was escape. I stood up with Eilene in my arms and headed as fast as I could to the nearest exit. For some strange reason, I did not grab Kathy's hand nor did she follow.

I went down to the steps and on to the sidewalk. Here I was in front of the church with Eilene, who was now energetically running around on the beautiful summery day thoroughly enjoying herself. I was miserable, humiliated, and thinking I was an impossibly bad mother not able to control her daughters at all and too stupid to gather Kathy and go home. I was a failure again. The church service seemed endless in my long wait. Finally the people came streaming out. Five year old Kathy was nonchalantly holding the hand of a parishioner who had taken her on and escorted her out of the church.

A very kindly man who was one of the trustees of the church came over to me. He was widely known to sleep through the whole Sunday service, so Eilene must have rudely awakened him from his snooze. The man spoke gently to Kathy and Eilene and then he said to me, "That's about the loudest Declaration of Independence I have ever heard." Truer words were never said. We all laughed.

So this is it. This is Eilene and our family--loud, obnoxious, and independent.

Don and Bev with Libby.

Don with Will.

NANCY

We had not planned to have a third child but we did. It was meant to be. How would we ever have managed our lives without Nancy?

I grew very large with the pregnancy. I outgrew my maternity clothes which were stretchy pants and large loose tops at the time. It was summer at the end. My sister-in-law, Wanda, who was an excellent seamstress made me a couple of tent dresses that I wore at the end.

On the Fourth of July Don and I, Eilene and Kathy attended a water event at Bass Lake near home. Prizes were award for attendance. I won a water belt which was to support me in the lake. It definitely was not long enough to switch around my middle in my present state. I actually made Don go up and accept it. I didn't want jokes and laughter.

A few days later I entered the hospital with labor pains. I was there for almost a day and they stopped. Because of my size and the size of the baby, Doctor Armstrong gave me a shot to start labor once more. It was often mentioned that I must be having a boy, because the birth was taking so long.

It was July and the oats had been cut for harvest. This was weighing on Don's mind and he wanted me to hurry up and have this child. He would stop in the hospital often and I could sense that his usual patience was not visible. There was definitely tension in the slow process of birth and he was torn between the oats and the baby.

He told me that our neighbors, Eileen and Jergy had been at the Legion the night before. Eileen had had a bit to drink and when they returned home Eileen had been asleep in the car. Jergy left her there and thought when she woke up that she would come in the house. It was morning before this occurred and although it was July, Eileen said she was about frozen. Actually she was certainly an omen that the baby was a boy.

Eventually the baby came and she was large, about ten and a half pounds. Toppin babies for some reason were often of great size. Both my sisters-in-law, Wanda and Liz, had babies in Nancy's range for weight. Her uncle, Harold, her Dad's oldest brother was also in the ten pound area. Big babies are well developed and easy to care for which was fortunate for me. However, I did not feel well after the birth although I had no severe medical problems. Mrs. Osborn, Juanita Hopp's mother, came out to the farm to help me. She was very efficient and Don admired her much for this. She cooked and left supper for us before she went home for the evening.

Efficiency is not among my virtues, but I became better and took over the household duties as best I could. Nancy was a good baby and slept well.

When she was about five months old strange red marks began to appear on her head and on her ear. I took her to Dr. Armstrong and he sent us to Mankato to a specialist. He told us that they were hematomas and would disappear in time. They consisted of a group of blood vessels which would eventually be cut off and the marks which had become bumps would be gone. Dr. Armstrong was a very good family physician and we had a good relationship with him.

He told me, "You know, if she were my daughter I would take her to Rochester for a second opinion." This we did.

We were concerned about paying for expensive medical care at the Mayo Clinic, the best medical facility in the United States, but we knew we had to do this. This was before health insurance had become a common necessity. When Nancy was brought in for her appointment, we had to give a full financial statement. Because we were tenant farmers and low income, it cost us only $15.00 to have her examined by a physician and a number of interns. They carefully measured the size of the bumps and wrote a description of them. They gave the same diagnosis as the Mankato specialist. The very red bumps were a collection of blood vessels which would eventually be deprived of their blood supply and would disappear. They wanted to be certain of this, however, and asked that we come back again to be sure they had not grown. We did this and were again charged only $10.00. They once again measured and examined the bumps and gave the same diagnosis. Again they wanted us to return to be sure. This we did. On that trip we walked in the elevator to the main floor and there was Mickey Mantel who was receiving treatment there. We were so stunned and shy that we did not even say hello. We were big baseball fans, too. Don and his brothers followed the Yankees intensely. This was one of our missed opportunities in life.

By this time people were asking about the bumps. They thought perhaps Nancy had hit her head coming up under a table. As she grew older, her blonde hair grew in thickly and I pulled it carefully across the top of her head and placed a barrette at the back. This worked well and alleviated some of my worries about attending school and being teased. The bumps continued to grow smaller and eventually disappeared as she entered school just as had been predicted.

Nancy and I were in a style show at the school when she was somewhere between two and three. She was attired in a bikini which was very cute on her pudgy body. Fortunately I was able to wear a dress. She was to hold my hand going down the ramp. This she refused to do and made her own way to the end. Her independent streak was mentioned to me by attendees of the show. Nancy asserted her independence early and it never left her.

Nancy entered school. Mrs. Lawson her first grade teacher thought she did not seem happy. We as a family were somewhat stressed by our financial circumstances. Nancy also seems to have my emotional makeup and she wanted to do well in school. Her older sisters had and she knew it was always expected of her as well. Maybe there were other factors also of which I'm not aware. Every year a first grade boy and girl were selected to accompany the homecoming queen. Earl Doolittle's daughter, Debbie, headed the committee to make the choice. Earl was Don's cousin. Debbie was seriously organized and a very good student and all around person, well-liked by almost everyone. Nancy was chosen as the first grader to accompany the candidates and the queen. I was not particularly happy about this, for many reasons. In my family, it was best not to stand out at all and if we must it should because of accomplishment, academic or creative. The Toppins, particularly our family, was not liked. There was much jealously. I don't think Nancy was delighted about being chosen either, but what could we do? She must have felt the hostility. Later she would say when the name Toppin was mentioned, the retort was "Yuk!" But we were what we were and we are what we are.

I thought Nancy had a slight lisp. It was my feelings of guilt perhaps because I felt I had not had enough time for her, because we had such a busy life. I had managed to land a teaching position in Amboy because an English teacher had left in the middle of the year. There should have been all kinds of red flags around this, but we needed the money badly. Don was able to take care of Nancy most of the time, but when spring planting began she had to go to a day care person. Donna Hicks was not a close friend, but I knew her well, and she was a warm person. Nancy ended up there on the days when Don could not care for her.

When Nancy started school, they had a speech therapist that travelled the schools in the area. I asked if she could see my daughter. Nancy seemed to like the therapist and enjoyed working with others in the group who probably had much worse problems. Nancy and I both agree now that she really didn't need the speech therapy, but it wasn't an awful experience either. She later went to the state speech contest to compete in the extemporaneous poetry category. She also graduated from the University of Minnesota with a degree in speech communication.

Nancy had a lot of competition in her class with Mark Loomis and Sara Nagel. She kept up well. When she took a social studies class in senior high in which Eilene was also enrolled, Mr. Smith, the teacher, said, "Now Eilene has some real competition." Nancy also received the highest score on a competitive math test, besting both Sara and Mark. Mark was later to receive a PHD and work for NASA.

There were of course incidents as well. When Kathy was home for the weekend and Nancy had to go back to school in the evening, we let her take the car. She was not supposed to be driving at night and did not have a lot of driving experience. She rolled the car. Fortunately she was not badly injured. She had a cut on her head which required some stitches, but she was all right. We did not think about concussions at that time. There were infractions galore. The sheriff had not been called. She should not have been driving at all. But it is a small town where some persons were overlooked by the law if the consequences of the mishap were not too great.

When the chemical dependency center opened in Winnebago, I was hired as lead tutor. That meant I was an employee of the Winnebago Schools. Richard Newkirk was then superintendent of schools. He was very Conservative and did not really believe in chemical dependency treatment. Religion was the answer. He was, however, quite congenial and believed in following the law, so we got along well. He liked Nancy. She was a good student and was mostly a good citizen. As her mother's daughter, she did argue with him, however, about some rules of the school. I think he rather liked that.

Nancy is also her father's daughter. She had as friends Sharon Lloyd and Sue Slama. They are both excellent people, but not perfect. In the spring of their senior year they made a trip to Fox Lake to a dance. Nancy was just seventeen. A law official stopped at their booth and checked their I.D.'s. They were not of age and cited for underage drinking. Nancy had gone to the bathroom and missed the ticket. She argued with the police saying she should have received a ticket too but since she had not been present she escaped without punishment. Her friend, Sue, had to go to court in Fairmont, the Martin County seat because Fox Lake was located in Martin County. Sue who was eighteen could write her own excuse. Nancy, however, was only seventeen and could not do the same. She wrote her own and signed my name. Jean Kortuem who knew what had happened told the school. Jean always knew every bit of gossip in the town. Her daughter had been in a lot of trouble herself. Her son, Mike was in the same class as Sue and Nancy.

Since Rich Newkirk was a friend of both Nancy and me, he allowed Nancy to drive his old pickup to the farm to tell her parents what had occurred. He also called me to tell me she would be coming. Again the consequences were not applied, because of our connections. It wasn't really fair, but we did not fight it either. Nancy was smart and lucky. She is the savvy one although all three of my daughters fit the category.

Don with Nicole.

GRATITUDE

I have often thought I am the most fortunate person I know. Where to begin is the question. First of all I had two educated parents. They earned their education overcoming extreme difficulties. My father escaped the Cloquet Fire at the age of thirteen. He worked on a dairy farm and took the Greyhound bus to graduate from Barnum High School. He managed to work his way through the University of Minnesota in the Department of Agriculture. My mother grew up on a subsistence farm as far in the woods as it is possible to be in Minnesota between Bemidji and International Falls. She managed to attend normal school and become an elementary teacher. My parents met. My father, due to the New Deal and the policies of FDR, obtained a job as County Agricultural Agent in Kandiyohi County and they had two children, my brilliant hardworking younger sister and me. They expected a great deal of us. My sister achieved. I really didn't, but I survived and I have had an unremarkable, but very satisfying life. Despite my conflicts, with especially my mother, I am very grateful to them for all they gave to me including my education. I am grateful to my mother for all the poetry she quoted to me and how she shaped my reading selections and how she did encourage me to do my best even if I never lived up to her wishes.

I am overwhelmingly grateful for the friends and the class I had at Willmar High School. They were intelligent, hardworking and kind. Shirley and Gloria studied much harder than I did and I benefited and learned from them.

Strangely I was the only one, originally, who went to college. They later finished degrees because of circumstances. I was lucky enough to attend the University of Minnesota and my education opened a world I didn't know existed. Somehow I graduated even though I wasn't a stellar student and I actually received a letter from a Superintendent of Schools for teaching job in Core Education in Winnebago. There I met my husband who is probably the only person who would put up with me. I had a lot of boyfriends, but I knew then that none of the relationships could work, not because of them but because of me.

I always thought that being poor as we were as tenant farmers that Don and I, even if we lived on love, were somewhat cursed. I now think it was a great blessing for me. I learned to live poor and be happy. I learned to live with the loathing of the community in which I lived. I had a number of strikes against me, my education, my liberal attitude, and something else I learned along the way. We were raising three daughters who were fortunately very healthy and very smart. I had an opportunity to work with a group of fifth graders in a Junior Great Books exploration. We read Ali Baba and the Forty Thieves. Probably it wouldn't be allowed these days. One of the questions presented in our teaching suggestions was "Why did people hate Ali Baba when he wasn't rich like the people the populace admired?" I will never forget the answer Jay, the grandson of our family doctor, gave. He said, "It was because they lived so well without it."

I give thanks for my ancestors who came to this country and coped with the cruel circumstances into which they were thrown. They were clever and kind and I owe so much to all of them. They gave me my supportive parents.

I am elated to have available to me the best music at least in this country, perhaps in the world. Few are as good as the Minnesota Symphony Orchestra. Also available to me is the Guthrie Theater and its magnificent productions.

I am also grateful to the great authors which I can so easily access. Thank you Fyodor Dostoevsky, Jane Austin, Halldor Laxness, and always the great American authors Scott Fitzgerald, John Steinbeck, Ernest Hemingway, Marianne Moore, Mary Oliver and on and on. Then of course, there are the movies.

I have unbelievable friends who put up with my moods and rages. I can't understand why they do, but they do and I love them for it. I cannot go on without mentioning the creative writing group which is as supportive and kind as my indescribable friends.

Although I don't always agree with the opinions of the citizens of the country in which I find myself, I have many ideas which inspire me and for which I will eternally give thanks. I have the freedom and the right given to me in the Bill of Rights to express my opinions. I don't know what would happen to me if I couldn't. Would I be stoned? Would I be killed in some other way? Would I be imprisoned? As it is, I am only condemned for the ideas which other people oppose. I receive hatred but not physical retaliation. I am grateful beyond words for this freedom. I am very grateful for Martin Luther King and the granting of Civil Rights that he brought to the country. But I am afraid for the steps toward justice and equality that the Civil Rights Act brought because Republicans do not respect or want Justice and equality. Will they ever consider justice for the Native Americans? Will they ever even keep, at this late date, the promises made in the treaties signed by the United States government?

I am very grateful for Freedom of Religion, but again I am afraid. The Religious Right or Alt Right or the white supremacists or whatever they are called do not believe that Moslems or Buddhists or Hindus or atheists or anyone with different beliefs should have any rights at all. I believe they will impose their will by outlawing abortion and gay rights and gay marriage. My beliefs and my church's beliefs are different from theirs. We will not be allowed to keep them. I know and am grateful for the Constitution of the United States and especially the Bill of Rights. But it appears to apply only to white Caucasians who believe as the Right Wing believes. I can pass as conventional probably if I slur my words and coarsen my language. How wonderful to have no more political correctness. I can call anyone anything I want to now that it has been abolished. It probably won't matter because I will probably be dead anyway, but my country, my church, and my beliefs are threatened.

Lastly of all I must say how grateful I am to my enemies. They show me who I am and where I need to stand. I am also grateful to those people who see me as I am and tolerate me anyway. Recently someone told me I had subtle sense of humor and also that I was really mean. How true! For whatever good or bad that is I am grateful. I love truth no matter how obscure and sometimes hurtful it is. Please help me to love my enemies and my neighbors as I do myself.

Made in the USA
Lexington, KY
03 June 2017